the ARTFUL Card

BY ALISON EADS

NORTH LIGHT BOOKS

CINCINNATI, OHIO
WWW.ARTISTSNETWORK.COM

09 08 07 06 05   5 4 3 2 1

Distributed in Canada by Fraser Direct
100 Armstrong Avenue
Georgetown, ON, Canada L7G 5S4
Tel: (905) 877-4411

Distributed in the U.K. and Europe by David & Charles
Brunel House, Newton Abbot, Devon, TQ12 4PU, England
Tel: (+44) 1626 323200, Fax: (+44) 1626 323319
Email: mail@davidandcharles.co.uk

Distributed in Australia by Capricorn Link
P.O. Box 704, S. Windsor NSW, 2756 Australia
Tel: (02) 4577-3555

Library of Congress Cataloging-in-Publication Data

Eads, Alison

   The artful card / Alison Eads.

      p. cm.

   Includes index.

   ISBN 1-58180-680-9

1. Greeting cards. I. Title.

TT872.E23 2005

745.594'1--dc22

                          2004027001

EDITOR Krista Hamilton

DESIGNER Marissa Bowers with assistance
              from Leigh Ann Lentz

LAYOUT ARTIST Jessica Schultz

PRODUCTION COORDINATOR Robin Richie

PHOTOGRAPHERS Hal Barkan
                 Al Parrish
                 Christine Polomsky

PHOTOGRAPHY STYLIST Janet A. Nickum

METRIC CONVERSION CHART

to convert	to	multiply by
Inches	Centimeters	2.54
Centimeters	Inches	0.4
Feet	Centimeters	30.5
Centimeters	Feet	0.03
Yards	Meters	0.9
Meters	Yards	1.1
Sq. Inches	Sq. Centimeters	6.45
Sq. Centimeters	Sq. Inches	0.16
Sq. Feet	Sq. Meters	0.09
Sq. Meters	Sq. Feet	10.8
Sq. Yards	Sq. Meters	0.8
Sq. Meters	Sq. Yards	1.2
Pounds	Kilograms	0.45
Kilograms	Pounds	2.2
Ounces	Grams	28.4
Grams	Ounces	0.04

ABOUT THE AUTHOR
Alison is a stay-at-home mom who has been quietly scrapbooking on her own for about seven years. As a self-proclaimed lover of "eye truffles" (like eye candy, only more so!), Alison feels that these special cards and keepsakes are gifts in themselves.

Her style has been honed through years of interest in the creative and decorative arts. Although she is a new face in the industry (this is her first published book), Alison has been exercising her creative muse for many years. She's danced, designed clothing and written everything from poetry to training programs. Alison is currently a designer and instructor for Scrapbook Central in West Chester, Ohio.

Alison and her adorable husband, Charlie, met and married in San Francisco and have called the Cincinnati area home for the last fifteen years. They have two practically perfect children and are busy living (mostly) happily ever after.

ACKNOWLEDGMENTS
Thank you to Tricia Waddell, Krista Hamilton, Christine Polomsky and everyone at North Light Books. You have made this an incredible experience.

Thanks, also, to my husband, Charlie, who has encouraged and supported me in every way. And to my children, who, for months, endured a mommy in a state of creative frenzy—you are the best!

DEDICATION
This book is dedicated to Patty Rose. Without her insistence, I would never have attempted this project. Patty sees what doesn't yet exist, then makes it happen. She nourishes creativity in herself and others and dreams bigger than anyone I know.

TABLE OF CONTENTS

BE EXTRAVAGANT!

SOMETIMES IT'S DIFFICULT TO ADEQUATELY EXPRESS OUR FEELINGS, TO LET THOSE WE CARE FOR THE MOST KNOW JUST HOW PRECIOUS THEY ARE. LET'S FACE IT, AN EMAIL JUST DOESN'T ALWAYS CUT IT. BUT GIVE A HANDMADE BIT OF ART, INFUSED WITH YOUR OWN PERSONALITY ... NOW WE'RE GETTING SOMEWHERE!

For me, the greatest pleasure in the paper arts is combining color, texture, images and text to create meaning and beauty. Each element contributes to the whole. It's also fun to see how many ways you can support your theme by your choice of materials and composition.

I would characterize the style of the cards and gifts in this book as collage, with a "cottage chic" sensibility. Collage is simply the process of gluing various materials onto a surface to create an artistic composition. We've all done similar stuff in grade school. As for the cottage chic part, you'll find a mix of modern and vintage, with elements that are classic, floral or just time-worn, combined with contemporary materials or settings. There are few constraints with this style, so allow yourself to play a bit. I want to encourage you to let your own personality come through. As you work and explore, push things a little bit. Go over the top once in a while. Be extravagant, whimsical or even (gasp) tacky. It will make you feel better.

When I get stuck and need a little inspiration, I'll often turn to fashion or home decorating magazines to recharge my creative batteries. Almost invariably, a color scheme or design will leap out and beg to be reinterpreted. I've always been a bit of a gypsy at heart, so I have a colorful design "vocabulary." Feel free to work with your own favorite colors and themes, and use the ideas in this book as a jumping-off place for your creative experimentation.

"Creativity is allowing yourself to make mistakes. Art is knowing which ones to keep."

SCOTT ADAMS

FRIENDS FOR ALL TIME

IT HAS BEEN SAID THAT GOOD FRIENDS ARE extensions of our true selves. To me, this means that they offer us a glimpse of other aspects of our own selves that we may not yet have imagined. How wonderful! With a true friend, we are able to explore the full range of our own possibility. C. S. Lewis once said, *"True friendship starts the moment one person says, 'What? You too? I thought I was the only one!'"* In some ways, it does feel like we "recognize" our friends when we meet them.

On the other hand, all seriousness aside, friends are fun. Goodness knows we all need opportunities to be zany, to look foolish, to try and to fail. That's where friends come in. Isn't it delicious to run pell-mell into the unknown alongside an equally heedless companion? There's a delirious sort of joy in that "what the heck, let's just try it" approach to life. Friendship touches all of the crucial elements of our lives. I think it is an intimate relationship partly because it encompasses so much— the mundane as well as the momentous. We may see our friends daily or once a decade. They can be new-found or the stalwart companions of childhood. They may join us on our path for a season or for a lifetime. They may be spouses, family members, classmates or co-workers. However they come into our lives, we treasure them.

Each of the projects in this chapter celebrates a different aspect of friendship, from the silly to the sublime.

TRUE METAMORPHOSIS

HAVE YOU EVER EXPERIENCED a friend's encouragement as you break through to a new stage in your life? A friend can take you by the hand as you attempt this sometimes scary metamorphosis. My friends have often been the ones who have helped me grow the most, so a butterfly card seemed a natural way to honor that aspect of friendship. The large scale of the vine paper looks great with the butterfly image, giving it a sense of proportion by highlighting the butterfly's tiny size and fragility. And the matchbook-style opening is unconventional, just like some of my favorite people.

"Each friend represents a world in us, a world possibly not born until they arrive."

ANAIS NIN

MATERIALS FOR TOP-FOLD CARD

Card: medium green cardstock cut to 4⅝" x 9½" (11.7cm x 24.1cm)

Light green cardstock cut to 4⅞" x 4¼" (12.4cm x 10.8cm)

Teal cardstock cut to 4" x 3" (10.2cm x 7.6cm)

Polka dot paper cut to 1½" x 4¾" (3.8cm x 12.1cm)

Medallion print paper cut to 4⅝" x 3⅞" (11.7cm x 9.8cm)

Leaf print paper cut to 3⅞" x 2⅞" (9.8cm x 7.3cm)

Text print paper torn to 2" x 1½" (5.1cm x 3.8cm)

Color copy of vintage butterfly image

One decorative brad

Off-white acrylic paint

Sewing machine or needle and light blue thread

Cutting, punching and scoring tools (see page 122 for options)

Adhesives (see page 122 for options)

POLKA DOT AND MEDALLION PRINT PAPERS BY K&COMPANY • LEAF PRINT PAPER BY PAPERWHITE MEMORIES • TEXT PRINT PAPER BY 7GYPSIES • VINTAGE BUTTERFLY IMAGE BY DOVER • BRAD BY MAKING MEMORIES

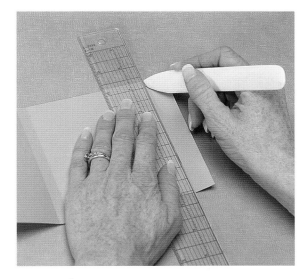 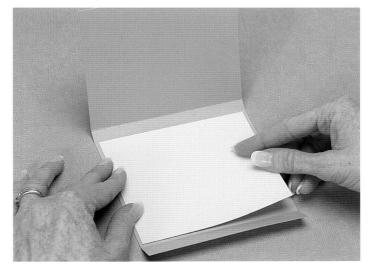

STEP 1 Position the medium green cardstock horizontally on your work surface. Measure over 4¼" (10.8cm), 4⅝" (11.7cm) and 8⅞" (22.5cm) from the left edge and mark the top and bottom with a pencil. Score, fold and crease as described on page 124.

STEP 2 Position the card vertically with the small flap at the bottom. Glue the light green cardstock to the panel above the small flap. This becomes the inside panel of the card.

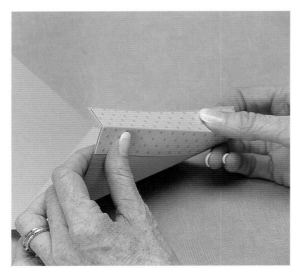

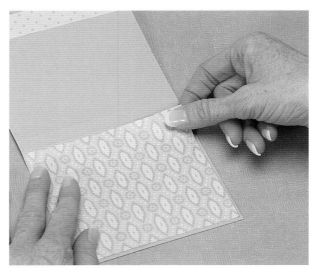

STEP **3** Fold the polka dot paper in half vertically and glue it to the outside bottom of the card, aligning the folds as shown.

STEP **4** Position the card with the inside panel face down and the small panel at the top. Glue the medallion print paper to the bottom flap. This becomes the front of the card. Close the card and set it aside for use in step 7.

STEP **5** Glue the leaf print paper to the teal cardstock, then glue the torn text print paper to the bottom left corner of the leaf print paper.

STEP **6** Trim the butterfly image with a craft knife and apply the image over the torn text print paper with glue dots. Cut a slit through the bottom right corner of the paper and cardstock. It should be large enough to accommodate the brad prongs.

⟡ STEP **7** Insert the brad prongs through the slit and bend them outward to secure the brad. Apply a dab of off-white acrylic paint to the face of the brad and smudge it around with your finger to antique it. Glue the layered butterfly piece to the front of the card, centered in all directions.

⟡ STEP **8** Use a sewing machine or needle and light blue thread to make a zigzag stitch across the bottom flap on the front of the card. Tuck the lower edge of the card's front panel behind the bottom flap to hold the card closed—just like a matchbook.

LAST MONARCH

With a change of color, this card can evoke an autumnal mood. I kept the butterfly theme, but instead of a paper butterfly image, I used a butterfly-shaped button that I covered with poppy-hued acrylic paint. I swiped the silk maple leaf with gold ink and highlighted it with a gold leafing pen. Instead of stitching the lower flap, I punched two holes and knotted some fibers to hold it closed and add a decorative touch.

SWEETNESS WITH A CHERRY ON TOP

I LOVE THIS PINK AND BROWN COLOR SCHEME! Doesn't it make you think of Neapolitan ice cream? It inspired me to create this fun collage card. Rusty Pickle makes great little file folder cards, which can be used as is, and also as templates for making file folder cards with your own decorative papers, as I have done here. With a few funky embellishments, including a vintage slide holder and dangling metal rim circle tag, this interactive card becomes a hip tribute to a special person. A layered sundae inside the folder makes this card perfect for the friend who adds sweetness to your life.

> *"We're quite a pair!*
> *You be Ethel,*
> *I'll be Lucy."*
>
> AUTHOR UNKNOWN

14

MATERIALS FOR TOP-FOLD CARD

Card: pink and brown striped cardstock cut to 7" x 10" (17.8m x 25.4cm), then folded to 7" x 5" (17.8cm x 12.7cm)

Pink and brown diamond print cardstock cut to 5" x 7" (12.7cm x 17.8cm)

Polka dot paper cut to 6" x 8½" (15.2cm x 21.6cm)

Ledger paper cut to 6" x 8½" (15.2cm x 21.6cm)

Ice cream print paper

Scraps of pink floral print and ledger papers cut to 1⅞" x 2" (4.8cm 5.1cm)

File folder card (used as template)

1¼" (3.2cm) metal rim circle tag

Three large eyelets

One spiral clip

One fabric flower with wire stem

One metal slide holder

3" (7.6cm) piece of pink gingham ribbon

3" (7.6cm) piece of white thread

5" (12.7cm) elastic cord

Foam alphabet and tiny alphabet stamps

Brown and pink pigment inks

Eyelet setter and hammer

Cutting, punching and scoring tools (see page 122 for options)

Adhesives (see page 122 for options)

STRIPED, POLKA DOT AND DIAMOND PRINT PAPERS AND FOAM ALPHABET STAMPS BY MAKING MEMORIES ✦ LEDGER PAPER AND ELASTIC CORD BY 7GYPSIES ✦ ICE CREAM PRINT PAPER BY MASTERPIECE STUDIOS ✦ PINK FLORAL PRINT PAPER BY DOODLEBUG DESIGNS ✦ FILE FOLDER CARD BY RUSTY PICKLE ✦ TINY ALPHABET STAMPS BY HERO ARTS ✦ METAL SLIDE HOLDER BY TRULY VINTAGE ✦ TAG BY AVERY

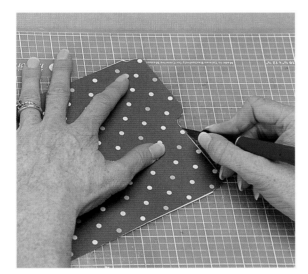

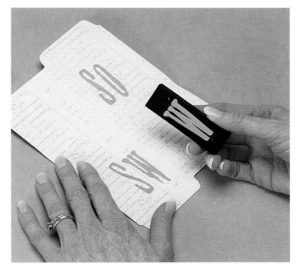

STEP 1 Using the file folder card as a template, trace it onto the front of the polka dot paper and the back of the ledger paper. Cut out the folder shapes and glue them back to back. Trim around the edges with a craft knife to tidy them up and make sure they are symmetrical. Score and fold the file folder as described on page 124 with the polka dot paper on the outside.

STEP 2 Apply pink acrylic paint to the foam alphabet stamps and stamp the phrase "So sweet!" on the inside of the file folder.

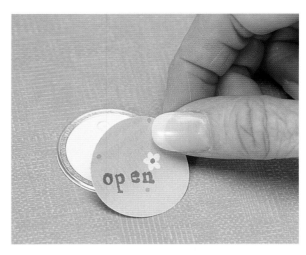

STEP 3 Cut out a few scoops from the ice cream print paper and glue them next to the word "so." Apply brown pigment ink to the tiny alphabet stamps and stamp the phrase "you are" onto a scrap of pink floral print paper. Trim the paper to the size of the folder tab and glue it in place.

STEP 4 Cut two 1¹⁄₄" (3.2cm) circles out of a scrap of pink floral print paper. Apply brown pigment ink to the tiny alphabet stamps and stamp the word "open" on one of the circles. Glue the circle to one side of the metal rim circle tag, then glue the remaining circle to the other side of the tag. Re-punch the hole in the tag.

STEP 5 Punch a hole in the top right corner of the file folder, just below the tab. Set an eyelet in the hole as described on page 124. Tie the circle tag through the eyelet with a piece of white thread. Close the file folder and set it aside for use in step 7.

STEP 6 Apply brown pigment ink to the tiny alphabet stamps and stamp the word "dolce" (that's Italian for "sweet") onto the scrap of pink floral print paper, then tear off and discard the top edge. Glue the piece to the bottom of the scrap of ledger paper, then insert the layered piece into the metal slide holder.

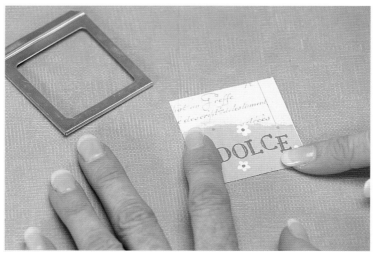

STEP 7 Pinch the pink gingham ribbon at the center and wrap the wire from the fabric flower around it. Trim the ribbon and excess wire, then glue the flower and ribbon to the slide mount with gel medium. Glue the slide mount to the front of the file folder. Set aside to dry.

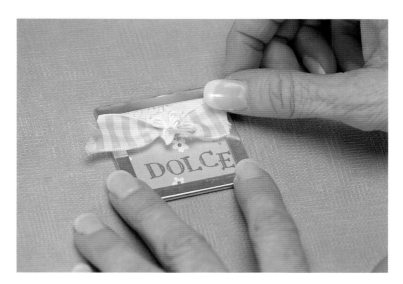

STEP 8 Tear the top left corner off the diamond print paper and discard the rest. Glue the diamond print corner to the upper right corner of the striped card. Punch diagonal holes on the front panel of the card and set eyelets in each hole as described on page 124.

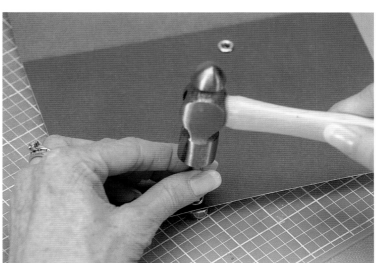

STEP 9 String the elastic cord through the eyelets and tie a knot at each end to secure. Slip the file folder under the elastic cord to hold it in place. Add the spiral clip at the top of the file folder.

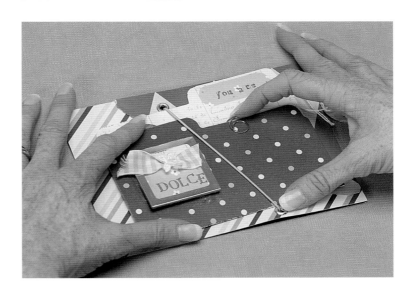

GIVE THE GIFT OF LAVENDER

I LOVE THE SMELL OF LAVENDER. It is clean and old-fashioned in a reassuring way. In my garden, I often plant lavender beneath my rosebushes. They get along well together, complementing each other in form and fragrance. Good friends often seem to work the same way, each enhancing the other. I vaguely recall an old proverb that says when you give a gift of flowers, some of the fragrance remains on your own hands. This card's beautiful colors and layers are further enhanced by the fragrance of the dried lavender sprigs. For mailing purposes, gently cover the card with bubble wrap or tissue paper and use a padded envelope to protect the fragile dried blossoms.

"Those who bring sunshine to the lives of others cannot keep it from themselves."

JAMES BARRIE

MATERIALS FOR SIDE-FOLD CARD

Card: dark gold cardstock cut to 10" x 7" (25.4cm x 17.8cm), then folded to 5" x 7" (12.7cm x 17.8cm)

Corrugated cardboard cut to 4" x 3½" (10.2cm x 8.9cm)

Eggplant cardstock torn to 5" x 7" (12.7cm x 17.8cm)

Eggplant cardstock cut to 1" x 3½" (2.5cm x 8.9cm)

Lavender print paper cut to 4⅛" x 6⅛" (10.5cm x 15.6cm) and ¾" x 3¼" (1.9cm x 8.3cm)

Scrap of white paper

One large shipping tag

One faux postage sticker

Four large eyelets

Three sprigs of dried lavender

Three 6"–9" (15.2cm to 12.9cm) pieces of purple and green fibers

8" (20.3cm) piece of hemp cord

Text stamp

Olive green pigment ink

Antique Linen distress ink

Olive green acrylic paint

Eyelet setter and hammer

Cutting, punching and scoring tools (see page 122 for options)

Adhesives (see page 122 for options)

DARK GOLD PAPER BY MAKING MEMORIES • LAVENDER PRINT PAPER BY CREATIVE IMAGINATIONS • TAG BY AVERY • STICKER BY EK SUCCESS (NOSTALGIQUES COLLECTION) • DISTRESS INK BY RANGER

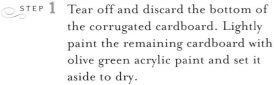

STEP **1** Tear off and discard the bottom of the corrugated cardboard. Lightly paint the remaining cardboard with olive green acrylic paint and set it aside to dry.

STEP **2** Glue the larger piece of lavender print paper to the larger piece of eggplant cardstock. Punch holes in all four corners through both layers and set eyelets in each of the holes as described on page 124.

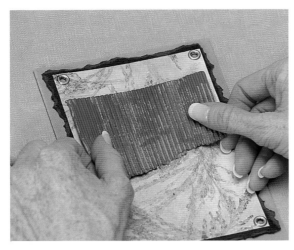

◯ STEP 3 Glue the layered eggplant and lavender print papers to the front of the dark gold card, then glue the painted cardboard over the lavender print paper with the top edge about 1" (2.5cm) from the top of the card.

◯ STEP 4 Print or write the phrase "thank you" across the smaller strip of lavender print paper, then tear off and discard the bottom right corner. Tear off the left and right sides of the small strip of eggplant paper. Layer the lavender strip over the eggplant strip, then glue the layered piece to the front of the card near the bottom.

TIP: USE A SCRAP PIECE OF PAPER TO PROTECT YOUR WORK SURFACE.

◯ STEP 5 Print or write the word "lavender" on a large shipping tag. Ink the text stamp with olive green pigment ink and stamp it onto the tag.

◯ STEP 6 Swipe the tag with Antique Linen distress ink to give it an aged look.

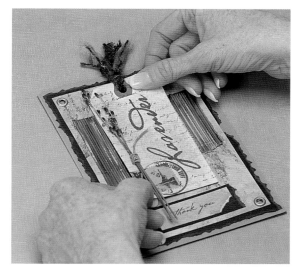

STEP **7** Apply the faux postage sticker to the bottom of the tag. Bundle up three lavender sprigs, tie the stems together with hemp cord and glue the bundle to the tag with a dab of gel medium.

STEP **8** Tie fibers through the hole in the top of the tag and glue it to the front of the card with gel medium. Trim the fibers and fluff as desired.

VINTAGE HALLOWEEN

You can do almost anything with a large shipping tag. Here, I covered the tag with patterned paper, then cut out a mosaic window. Vintage Halloween-themed paper provided images to layer behind the window. I also used them to create a torn-paper background. To give the card a worn, scruffy appearance, I swiped the edges with distress ink.

RETAIL THERAPY

RETAIL THERAPY

A NEW LOOK

Misses' and Girls' Embroidered Hats

LET'S GO SHOPPING

I LOVE TO SHOP, and shopping with a friend is even better! This card combines girly elements, like the pink and green color scheme, rhinestones and hairpin embellishments, with some edgier stuff, like the black harlequin print paper and label tape text. I've also combined retro images with bits that are more contemporary. To me, the juxtaposition of components lends excitement and energy to this collage card. It is quirky and individual. And that works in fashion as well as in friendship!

"Give a girl the right pair of shoes and she can conquer the world."

BETTE MIDLER

MATERIALS FOR TOP-FOLD CARD

Card: lime sparkle cardstock cut to 6" x 12" (15.2cm x 30.5cm), then folded to 6" x 6" (15.2cm x 15.2cm)

Foam core cut to 4" x 4" (10.2cm x 10.2cm)

Pink sponged paper cut to 5⅞" x 5⅞" (14.9cm x 14.9cm)

Black and cream diamond print paper cut to 5½" x 5½" (14cm x 14cm)

Black text print paper cut to 3¾" x 3¾" (9.5cm x 9.5cm)

Pink mulberry paper cut to 3½" x 6" (8.9cm x 15.2cm)

Lime embossed paper cut to 4¼" x 4½" (10.8cm x 11.4cm)

Collage print paper

Vintage image or color copy of photo

Four black photo corners

Three blue rhinestones

Two black hairpins

Label maker and label tape

Cutting, punching and scoring tools (see page 122 for options)

Adhesives (see page 122 for options)

PINK SPONGED PAPER BY EK SUCCESS ◆ BLACK AND CREAM DIAMOND PRINT PAPER BY GIFTED LINE ◆ BLACK TEXT PRINT PAPER BY 7GYPSIES ◆ LIME EMBOSSED PAPER BY K&COMPANY ◆ COLLAGE PRINT PAPER BY DESIGN ORIGINALS (MOM'S SEWING BOX COLLECTION) ◆ VINTAGE IMAGE BY ARTCHIX STUDIO ◆ LABEL MAKER AND LABEL TAPE BY DYMO

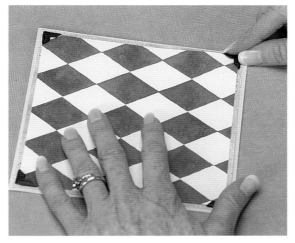

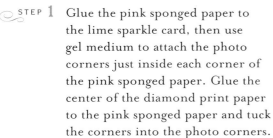

STEP 1   Glue the pink sponged paper to the lime sparkle card, then use gel medium to attach the photo corners just inside each corner of the pink sponged paper. Glue the center of the diamond print paper to the pink sponged paper and tuck the corners into the photo corners.

STEP 2   Tear the mulberry paper into an irregular shape and glue it to diamond print paper, then glue the lime embossed paper over the mulberry paper, centered in all directions. Fluff out the edges of the mulberry paper.

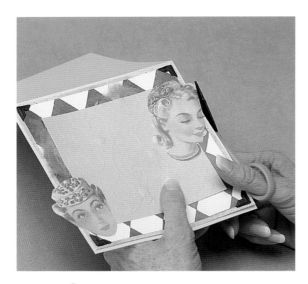

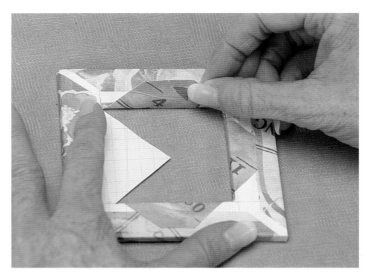

STEP **3** Cut out a few faces from the collage print paper, glue them to the front of the card and trim the excess from the sides. Set the card aside for use in step 6.

STEP **4** Trim the remaining collage print paper to 5½" x 5½" (14cm x 14cm). Cut a window measuring 2½" x 2½" (6.4cm x 6.4cm) in the center of the foam core. Apply gel medium to one side of the foam core and glue it to the collage print paper. Trim off the corners of the paper and wrap the remaining flaps around the foam core. Cut an X in the paper covering the window. Fold the flaps through the window and glue them to the foam core, trimming if necessary.

STEP **5**

Glue the vintage image or a color copy of a photo to the black text print paper diagonally, then glue the foam core frame over the image, as shown.

STEP **6** Use the label maker to spell out phrases related to shopping. I used "retail therapy," "a new look" and "let's go shopping." Stick the labels to the front of the card around the edges. Glue the framed image to the front of the card, then glue rhinestones and hair pins around the frame with gel medium.

FASHIONABLE FRIENDS

Not done shopping yet? The lovely ladies on this card were simply torn from patterned paper. I layered them over a crumpled, sanded wallpapery-looking background and added a torn train schedule, trimmed rose paper and a calendar sticker. To accessorize, I made a simple embellishment with tulle, ribbon and a shoe charm.

TO MAKE JOY

Here is my take on a "potion" for adding joy to your life. This card uses a foam core frame to showcase three tiny bottles filled with beads and glitter. Inked tags are tied to the bottles with fibers. For one bottle, I cut a small piece of patterned tissue paper, tied it around the opening and trimmed it.

THIS IDEA STARTED OUT as the cover of a small memory book, and it transformed into a cute card with lots of three-dimensional flair. Each of the letters is its own element. They combine into a whole for the title, much like different elements combine in life to form a friendship. It might be fun to create a different card for each of your special friends. You can personalize each card by including colors and embellishments that represent your friendship.

"You'll always be my best friend. You know too much."

AUTHOR UNKNOWN

MATERIALS FOR SIDE-FOLD CARD

Card: white cardstock cut to 12" x 6" (30.5cm x 15.2cm), then folded to 6" x 6" (15.2cm x 15.2cm)

Pink and white floral print paper cut to 5⅞" x 5⅞" (14.9cm x 14.9cm)

Aqua swirl paper

Scrap of white paper

Mini file folder

Two 1¼" (3.2cm) metal rim circle tags and one tiny price tag

Letter stickers

Wooden letter "F"

Letters "L" and "T" brads

Letters "E" and "S" game tiles

One large puzzle piece

Three pink paper daisies

One hot pink rhinestone

6" (15.2cm) pieces of sheer pink, pink grosgrain, aqua grosgrain and dyed silk ribbons

White thread (or string from tag)

Foam alphabet, tiny alphabet, daisy and swirl stamps

Pink and black pigment inks

Black permanent ink

Light teal and white acrylic paints

Cutting, punching and scoring tools (see page 122 for options)

Adhesives (see page 122 for options)

PINK AND WHITE FLORAL PRINT PAPER BY CHATTERBOX ◆ AQUA SWIRL PAPER BY PROVO CRAFT ◆ MINI FILE FOLDER BY DMD (PAPER REFLECTIONS COLLECTION) ◆ TAGS BY AVERY ◆ STICKERS BY CREATIVE IMAGINATIONS, REBECCA SOWER DESIGNS AND DAISY D'S ◆ WOODEN LETTER BY MICHAEL'S ◆ LETTER BRADS BY COLORBÖK ◆ LETTER CHARMS, ALPHABET STAMPS AND DAISY BLOSSOMS BY MAKING MEMORIES ◆ TINY ALPHABET STAMPS BY HERO ARTS ◆ DAISY STAMP BY STAMP DÉCOR ◆ RIBBONS BY OFFRAY, MIDORI AND 7GYPSIES

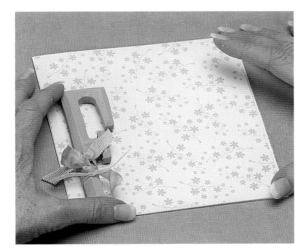

STEP 1 Paint the wooden letter "F" with light teal acrylic paint and allow it to dry. Tie pink and aqua grosgrain ribbons around the letter in individual bows and trim the ends to about 1" (2.5cm). Glue the pink and white floral print paper to the front of the white card, then glue the wooden letter to the bottom left corner with gel medium.

STEP 2 Apply pink pigment ink to the foam alphabet stamps and stamp "riend" following the wooden letter "F." Apply letter stickers over the stamped letters.

STEP 3 Apply light teal acrylic paint to the daisy stamp and stamp it randomly onto the pink and white floral print paper. Swipe a metal rim circle tag with pink pigment ink. Ink the tiny alphabet stamps with black permanent ink and stamp "ship" on the tag. Loop the pink and blue blended ribbon through the hole in the tag and glue it to the bottom right corner of the card. Add a pink paper daisy to the tag.

STEP 4 Swipe another metal rim circle tag with light teal acrylic paint. Glue a pink paper daisy to the tag with gel medium, then apply the letter "E" sticker, allowing it to hang off the bottom. Tie the sheer pink ribbon through the hole in the tag and attach the tag to the top left corner of the card with gel medium.

STEP 5

Swipe a tiny price tag with pink pigment ink and poke the letter "L" brad through the center of the tag. Bend back the prongs to secure the brad. Use gel medium to attach the tag, then the letter "E" game tile, to the card.

STEP 6

Swipe the puzzle piece with pink pigment ink, then apply letter "M," "E" and "N" stickers. Glue a pink paper daisy to the puzzle piece with gel medium, then attach the piece to the card.

STEP 7

Poke the letter "T" brad through the card and bend back the prongs, then glue a rhinestone to the letter "S" game tile and attach it to the card.

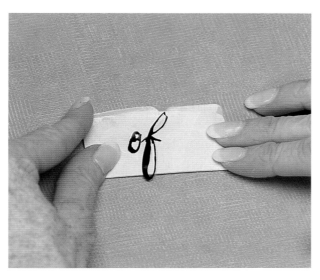

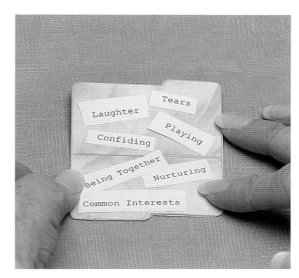

STEP **8** Swipe pink pigment ink onto the inside of the tiny file folder. Glue the aqua paper to the outside of the folder and trim off the excess. Apply white acrylic paint to the swirl stamp and stamp it onto the aqua paper on the folder. Allow the paint to dry, then apply "of" letter stickers to the folder.

STEP **9** Print or write friendship sayings on a scrap of white paper and cut them into tiny strips. Glue the strips to the inside of the file folder.

STEP **10** Glue a piece of white thread to the back of the file folder with the ends of the thread extending out from the top and bottom. Use gel medium to attach the file folder to the front of the card under the word "Elements."

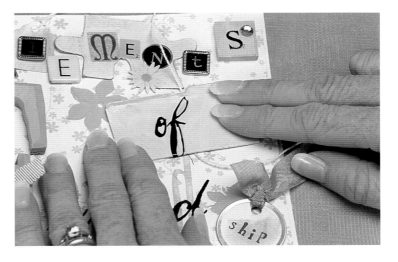

STEP **11** Tie the thread extending from the file folder into a bow and trim off the excess.

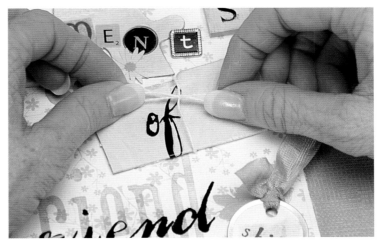

EVERYDAY PLEASURES

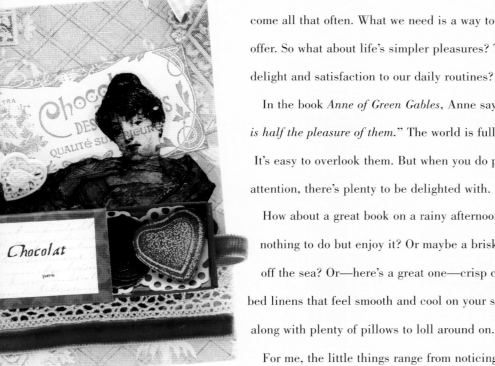

Some of the great joys in life are the big moments: first love, marriage and the birth of a child. These events are huge, transcendent, the crescendo of the symphony. The only trouble is, they don't come all that often. What we need is a way to enjoy the rest of what life has to offer. So what about life's simpler pleasures? Those everyday things that add delight and satisfaction to our daily routines?

In the book *Anne of Green Gables*, Anne says, *"Looking forward to things is half the pleasure of them."* The world is full of small, everyday pleasures. It's easy to overlook them. But when you do pay attention, there's plenty to be delighted with.

How about a great book on a rainy afternoon and nothing to do but enjoy it? Or maybe a brisk wind off the sea? Or—here's a great one—crisp clean bed linens that feel smooth and cool on your skin, along with plenty of pillows to loll around on.

For me, the little things range from noticing the light change in the garden as a storm moves in to having great conversations with my family. And there are even simpler pleasures to be had, if we take the time to notice.

For instance, I love to savor things like a great cup of coffee or tea in the afternoon, or an exquisite chocolate or luscious cake anytime. Just for fun, I've chosen to create projects that celebrate some of my favorite everyday pleasures. Enjoy these, then create your own!

COFFEE: CREATIVE LIGHTER FLUID

PEOPLE ARE SO PASSIONATE ABOUT COFFEE. For some, its power to revive and energize verges on the mystical. For this card, I wanted to capture a little of that in a playful way. Of course, I had to use a rich brown color in a card celebrating coffee. Layering pale blue over the brown brings the composition to life, and the addition of the cream color is for those of us who like our coffee to be more like dessert. Use your favorite roast for the coffee bean embellishment, but don't be tempted to use it in a cup!

"Behind every successful woman is a substantial amount of coffee."

STEPHANIE PIRO

MATERIALS FOR TOP-FOLD CARD

Card: light blue cardstock cut to 5" x 10" (12.7cm x 25.4cm), then folded to 5" x 5" (12.7cm x 12.7cm)

Paisley paper cut to 4³/₄" x 4³/₄" (12.1cm x 12.1cm)

Striped paper cut to 1³/₈" x 4³/₄" (3.5cm x 12.1cm)

Polka dot paper cut to 2¹/₂" x 1¹/₂" (6.4cm x 3.8cm)

Text print paper cut to 1¹/₂" x 1¹/₂" (3.8cm x 3.8cm)

Cream embossed paper cut to 2¹/₂" x 2¹/₂" (6.4cm x 6.4cm)

Scrap of light blue cardstock

Clear acetate

Vintage coffee and faux postage labels

One coffee bean

Three tiny round brown beads

Daisy and five-petal flower punches

5" (12.7cm) piece of light blue grosgrain ribbon

Coffee mug and corner scroll stamps

Brown pigment ink

Clear embossing powder

Off-white and light blue acrylic paints

Heat embossing tool

Sewing machine or needle and white thread

Cutting, punching and scoring tools (see page 122 for options)

Adhesives (see page 122 for options)

PAISLEY, POLKA DOT AND STRIPED PAPERS BY MAKING MEMORIES ◆ TEXT PRINT PAPER BY 7GYPSIES ◆ FAUX POSTAGE AND VINTAGE COFFEE LABEL BY ME AND MY BIG IDEAS ◆ FLOWER PUNCHES BY EK SUCCESS AND MARVY UCHIDA ◆ COFFEE MUG STAMP BY ART IMPRESSIONS ◆ RIBBON BY MIDORI

STEP 1 Glue the paisley paper to the front of the light blue card. Apply light blue acrylic paint to the corner scroll stamp and stamp it onto the bottom left corner of the paisley paper.

STEP 2 Print or write a coffee-related phrase on the striped paper. I used "Coffee: Creative Lighter Fluid." Glue the striped paper across the top of the card. Tear off the bottom right corners of the text print, cream embossed and polka dot papers. Glue them to the bottom right corner of the card, as shown. Set the card aside for use in step 6.

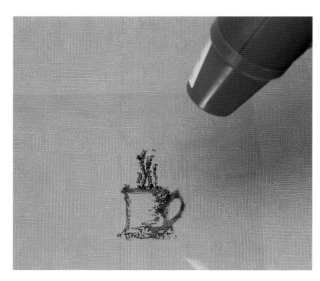

STEP 3 Ink the coffee mug stamp with brown pigment ink, stamp it onto a piece of clear acetate and sprinkle the wet ink with embossing powder. Pour the excess powder back into the container.

STEP 4 Heat the coffee mug image with the heat embossing tool to melt the embossing powder. This will add texture to the card and keep the ink from smudging.

STEP 5 Flip the acetate over and paint an irregular splotch of off-white acrylic paint over the coffee mug image. This will make it "pop."

STEP 6 Cut out an irregular shape around the coffee mug image and place it on the card, sliding the acetate under the striped paper at the top of the card if needed.

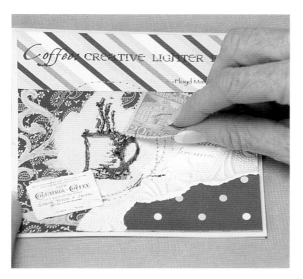
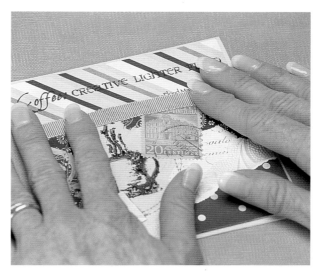

STEP **7** Open the card and use a sewing machine or needle and white thread to sew the coffee mug image to the front panel. Glue the coffee label and faux postage to the card on either side of the coffee mug.

STEP **8** Use gel medium to glue the light blue ribbon across the front of the card, just under the striped paper.

STEP **9** Punch three five-petal flowers and three daisies out of a scrap of light blue cardstock. Layer each daisy over a five-petal flower and bend up the petals to give them dimension. Use gel medium to glue a brown bead in the center of each flower.

STEP **10** Glue the flowers to the card as desired, then glue the coffee bean to the upper left corner of the card with gel medium.

I ONCE HEARD TEA DESCRIBED as a civilized response to an uncivilized world. Couldn't we all use some of that? I went through a period when I made myself tea nearly every afternoon, usually with a selection of sandwiches and cake or scones. I brewed my tea in a pot that belonged to my grandmother and arranged a tray with linen napkins and beautiful teacups. It was wonderfully indulgent and always felt like a treat. This card brings to mind the nostalgia of another era, when ladies in ravishing hats met to linger, and maybe gossip, over a cup of tea.

"Women are like tea bags...you don't know how strong they are until you get them into hot water."

ELEANOR ROOSEVELT

MATERIALS FOR SIDE-FOLD CARD

Card: dark gold cardstock cut to 10" x 7½" (25.4cm x 19.1cm), then folded to 5" x 7½" (12.7cm x 19.1cm)

Two pieces of cardboard cut to 1" x 1" (2.5cm x 2.5cm)

Medium olive cardstock cut to 4⅛" x 6⅜" (10.5cm x 16.2cm)

Dark olive cardstock torn to 5" x 7¼" (12.7cm x 18.4cm)

Light gold scroll pattern paper cut to 3⅞" x 5" (9.8cm x 12.7cm)

Flowers and butterflies collage paper cut to 3⅞" x 6⅛" (9.8cm x 15.6cm)

Scraps of flowers and butterflies collage paper and dark gold cardstock

Color copy of woman image

Letter and number stickers

Metal clock face and hands

One paper daisy blossom

One decorative button

One large brad

Tiny alphabet stamps

Metallic rub-ons

Green pigment ink

Walnut ink in spray bottle

Embossing ink

Clear embossing powder

Heat embossing tool

Cutting, punching and scoring tools (see page 122 for options)

Adhesives (see page 122 for options)

SCROLL PATTERN PAPER BY SCRAP-EASE • FLOWERS AND BUTTERFLIES COLLAGE PAPER BY K&COMPANY • STICKERS BY CREATIVE IMAGINATIONS (SONNETS COLLECTION) • WOMAN IMAGE BY DOVER (OLD TIME VIGNETTES CLIPART) • METAL CLOCK FACE AND HANDS BY JEST CHARMING EMBELLISHMENTS • DAISY BLOSSOM BY MAKING MEMORIES • TINY ALPHABET STAMPS BY HERO ARTS

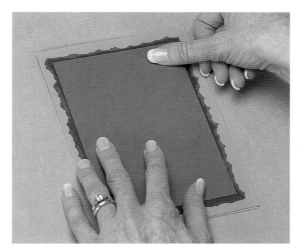

STEP 1 Glue the torn dark olive cardstock to the front of the dark gold card, then glue the medium olive cardstock to the dark olive cardstock.

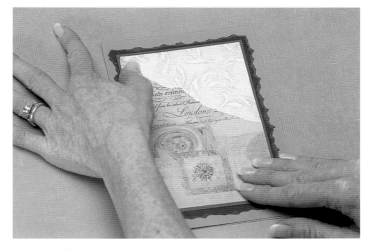

STEP 2 Glue the scroll pattern paper to the medium olive cardstock. Tear off and discard the top right corner of the flowers and butterflies collage paper and glue the remaining paper to the bottom left corner of the scroll pattern paper.

TIP: WHEN HEATING
SMALL PIECES OF PAPER, IT
HELPS TO HOLD THEM DOWN
WITH YOUR CRAFT KNIFE
OR TWEEZERS TO AVOID
BURNING YOUR FINGERS.

STEP 3 Tear out flower stem, butterfly and flower images from a scrap of flowers and butterflies collage paper. Swipe clear embossing ink over the stem, then emboss as described on page 34, steps 3 and 4.

STEP 4 Glue the butterfly, flower and embossed flower stem to the front of the card, overlapping them if desired.

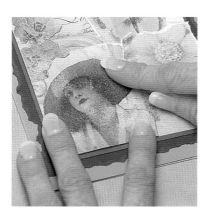

STEP 5

Cut out and emboss the woman image, then glue the image to the bottom left corner of the card. Set the card aside to dry.

STEP 6

Glue the two pieces of cardboard to the back of leftover scrap of flowers and butterflies collage paper. Cut around the pieces, trim off the corners and wrap the remaining flaps around the back of the cardboard to make tiles.

STEP 7

Emboss the cardboard tiles, then glue them to the card near the top right corner, as shown.

38

STEP 8 Use green pigment ink and tiny alphabet stamps to stamp the phrase "time for" onto a scrap of dark gold cardstock. Trim around each word and glue it to the clock face. Use gel medium to attach the clock face to the card below the tiles.

STEP 9 Punch a hole in the center of the card's front panel. Position the clock hands over the hole, insert a brad into the hole and bend the prongs outward to secure.

STEP 10

Distress the number "4" sticker and apply it to the front of the card below the clock face. Then, apply letter stickers to spell the word "tea" in the bottom right corner of the card.

STEP 11

Spray the paper daisy blossom with walnut ink to darken it. Use wire cutters or clippers to cut the shank off the button if necessary, then apply metallic rub-ons to the button and smudge it with your finger. Glue the button to the center of the paper daisy blossom with a dab of gel medium.

STEP 12

Attach the paper daisy blossom to the bottom left corner of the card with gel medium.

WHEN MY HUSBAND TRAVELED to Belgium on business, I made certain he knew that chocolate would be an appropriate gift to bring home for me. A good chocolate should be rich, luxurious, beautiful and preferably European. I've always believed that the ideal chocolate eating experience should be just a tad selfish, too. After all, who wants to share? This card is intended to evoke that feeling of pampered luxury. Embossing the candy pieces gives them a shiny finish, much like the satiny sheen on real chocolates.

"What you see before you, my friend, is the result of a lifetime of chocolate."

KATHARINE HEPBURN

40

MATERIALS FOR HANGING CARD

Cardboard cut to 4" x 5³⁄₄"
(10.2cm x 14.6cm)

Ivory cardstock

Pink toile print paper cut to
5¹⁄₂" x 7" (14cm x 17.8cm)

Tiny script paper cut to
1³⁄₄" x 1¹⁄₈" (4.5cm x 2.9cm)

Cranberry lattice print paper cut
to 2¹⁄₈" x 5" (5.4cm x 12.7cm)

Scraps of pink, dark brown
and tan papers

Clear self-adhesive shelf liner

Photocopy of woman image

One small matchbox

Two large flower eyelets

12" (30.5cm) piece of khaki
checked ribbon

5¹⁄₂" (14cm) pieces of pink
velvet and ivory crochet ribbons

Assorted fibers and buttons

Chocolate label, chocolate heart
and swirl candy stamps

Burgundy and dark brown pigment inks

Dark red acrylic paint

Clear embossing powder

Heat embossing tool

Eyelet setter and hammer

Cutting, punching and scoring
tools (see page 122 for options)

Adhesives (see page 122 for
options)

PINK TOILE PRINT PAPER BY
ANNA GRIFFIN, INC ✦ TINY SCRIPT
PAPER BY 7GYPSIES ✦ CRANBERRY
LATTICE PRINT PAPER BY
CREATIVE IMAGINATIONS (SONNETS
COLLECTION) ✦ WOMAN IMAGE
BY DOVER ✦ FLOWER EYELETS
BY DRITZ ✦ STAMPS BY RUBBER
BABY BUGGY BUMPERS ✦ RIBBON
BY MIDORI

TIP: TO DRY A PIECE
FLAT, PLACE SOMETHING
HEAVY, LIKE A BOOK,
ON TOP OF IT.

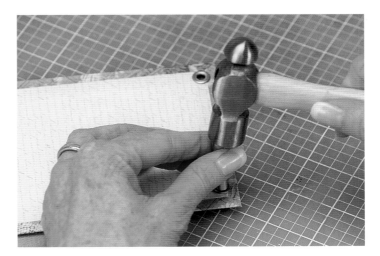

STEP 1 Apply a thin coat of gel medium
to one side of the cardboard and
glue it to the back of the pink toile
print paper. Trim off the corners
of the paper, fold over the remaining flaps and glue them to the
cardboard. Glue the tiny script
paper to the uncovered cardboard
as a backing piece. Allow to dry.

STEP 2 Punch holes in the upper corners of the
covered cardboard. You may need to do this a
few times to get the anywhere punch through
the thick cardboard. Set eyelets in the holes as
described on page 124.

STEP **3** Ink the chocolate label stamp with burgundy pigment ink and stamp it onto the ivory cardstock. Trim around the edges of the stamped image and drag the edges through the ink. Set aside to dry.

STEP **4** Thread the khaki checked ribbon through the eyelets in the covered cardboard and tie it in a bow. Glue the stamped chocolate label to the front of the cardboard near the top, then set the piece aside for use in step 11.

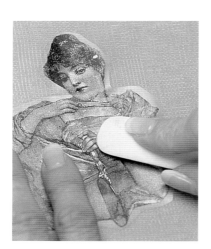

STEP **5**

Attach the woman image to the sticky side of the self-adhesive shelf liner. Trim around the edges and rub the image with a bone folder to smooth it. Submerge the image into water and allow it to soak for about five minutes.

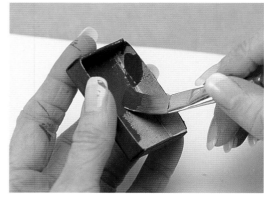

STEP **6** While the image is soaking, paint the inside and outside of the matchbox "drawer" with dark red acrylic paint and allow it to dry.

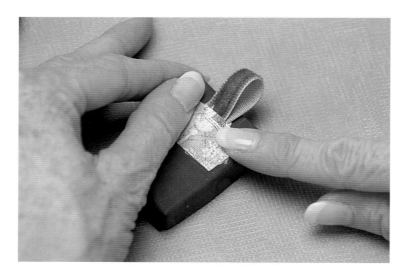

STEP **7**

When the drawer is dry, glue a 1" (2.5cm) piece of crochet trim to the inside bottom of the drawer to line it. Turn the drawer over. Loop a 1" (2.5cm) piece of pink velvet ribbon and glue both ends to the bottom of the drawer. This becomes a pull-tab. Cover the ends of the ribbon with a scrap of pink paper and glue in place. Set the excess crochet trim and ribbon aside for use in step 11.

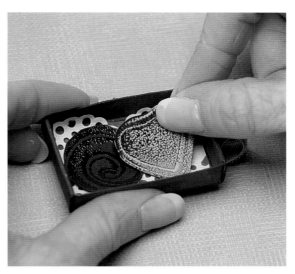

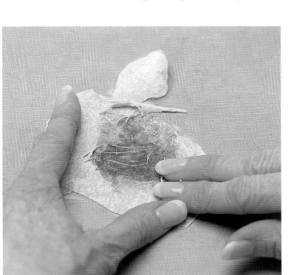

STEP **8** Coat the matchbox cover with gel medium, cover it with cranberry lattice paper and trim off the excess. Print or write the word "chocolat" on a piece of tiny script paper, trim it to the size of the matchbox top and glue it in place.

STEP **9** Ink the chocolate candy stamps with dark brown pigment ink. Stamp the heart candy stamp onto tan cardstock and the swirl candy stamp onto brown cardstock. Emboss the images as described on page 34, steps 3 and 4. Cut out the candy pieces and secure them inside the drawer with dimensional adhesive dots.

STEP **10**

Remove the woman image from the water and rub it with your fingers until the paper is completely removed from the shelf liner. (Don't rub too vigorously or you may remove some of the image.)

STEP **11**

Glue the transferred woman image to the covered cardboard from step 4, then glue the remaining crochet trim and velvet ribbon over the bottom of the image. To finish, glue the matchbox cover to the cardboard beside the woman image, insert the drawer and add various fibers and buttons as desired.

I ADORE BAKED GOODS AND LOVE TO COOK, but it was the quote, *"A good cook is like a sorceress who dispenses happiness,"* that really inspired this piece. Let's face it, making good food is a bit like magic. The whole feeling of this project is fun, from the housewife in her pearls and apron to the tiny milk bottles lining the front of the frame. The cherry plaid paper provides a retro color scheme, and the chenille rickrack and vintage labels play up the mood. You could also create this piece in colors that complement your kitchen, and perhaps even use a recipe that is special to your own family.

"The only way to get rid of temptation is to yield to it."

OSCAR WILDE

MATERIALS FOR FRAMED COLLAGE

7³/₈" x 7" (18.7cm x 17.8cm) wooden shadowbox frame

Foam core cut to 2¹/₂" x 6" (6.4cm x 15.2cm) and 2¹/₂" x 4³/₈" (6.4cm x 11.1cm)

White cardstock

Four strips of black and white gingham paper cut to 1" x 8" (2.5cm x 20.3cm)

Four strips of heart print paper cut to 1¹/₂" x 12" (3.8cm x 30.5cm)

Cherry plaid paper cut to 6⁷/₈" x 6¹/₂" (17.5cm x 16.5cm)

Green print paper cut to 2¹/₈" x 5¹/₄" (5.4cm x 13.3cm)

Cook image

Page from an old cookbook

Canned peas and vintage nutmeg container labels

Four heart and cherry buttons

Letters "C," "A," "K" and "E" wooden game tiles

Mini kitchen utensils

One small matchbox

7¹/₂" (19.1cm) piece of crochet trim

Four 7" (17.8cm) pieces of light green chenille rickrack trim

White acrylic paint

Sewing machine or needle and red thread

Cutting, punching and scoring tools (see page 122 for options)

Adhesives (see page 122 for options)

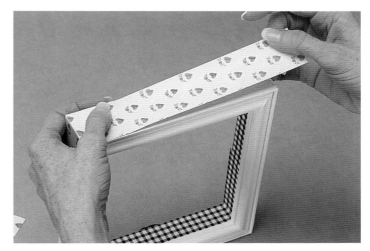

HEART PRINT PAPER BY COLORBÖK (TRACY PORTER COLLECTION) ◆ CHERRY PLAID PAPER BY ART IMPRESSIONS (SUSAN BRANCH COLLECTION) ◆ GINGHAM PAPER BY FRANCES MEYER ◆ GREEN PRINT PAPER AND VINTAGE NUTMEG CONTAINER LABEL BY K&COMPANY (VINTAGE LABELS COLLECTION) ◆ CANNED PEAS CONTAINER LABEL BY LI'L DAVIS DESIGNS ◆ COOK IMAGE BY DMD (PAPER REFLECTIONS COLLECTION) ◆ MINI KITCHEN UTENSILS BY JOLEE'S BOUTIQUE ◆ BUTTONS BY BLUMENTHAL LANSING CO ◆ RICKRACK TRIM BY WRIGHT'S

STEP 1 Remove the frame backing and paint the front of the frame with white acrylic paint. Don't worry too much about neatness because most of the frame will be covered with paper. Paint the outside of the matchbox drawer with white acrylic paint, as well, and allow both pieces to dry. Glue strips of gingham paper to the insides of the frame.

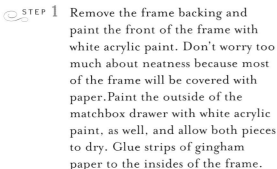

STEP 2 Cover the outside surface of the frame with strips of heart print paper. Set the frame aside for use in step 8.

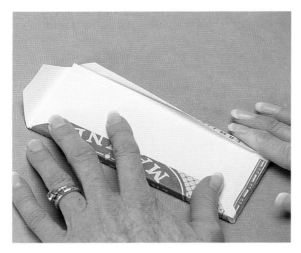

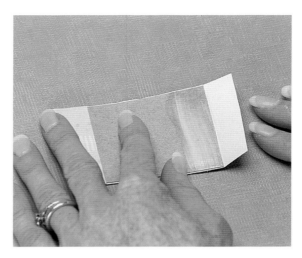

STEP **3** Glue the nutmeg container label to the small piece of foam core. Trim off the corners, fold over the flaps and glue them to the back of the foam core. Repeat with the large foam core and peas container label.

STEP **4** Cut off one of the narrow sides of the matchbox cover so it looks like an unbound book. Coat the outside of the book with gel medium, cover it with green print paper and trim off the excess. This becomes your cookbook cover.

STEP **5**

Retrieve the matchbox drawer from step 1 and glue it inside the cookbook cover. Print or write the words "Cookery Essentials" on a small piece of white cardstock, trim around the words and glue it to the front of the cookbook. Set aside to dry.

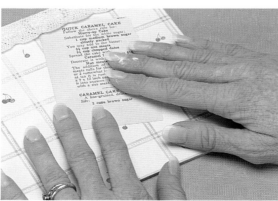

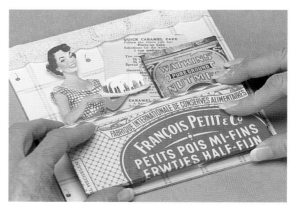

STEP **6** Cover the frame backing with cherry plaid paper, then glue the crochet trim across the top. Glue a page out of an old cookbook to the center of the cherry plaid paper, tilting it diagonally and tucking the top left corner under the trim.

STEP **7** Glue the cook image and nutmeg container label side by side over the cookbook page. Then, glue the peas container label across the entire backing piece, as shown.

STEP 8 Print or write several kitchen-related phrases on white cardstock and cut around them. I used the quote, "A good cook is like a sorceress who dispenses happiness," and cut it into three phrases. Stitch around the words with a sewing machine or needle and red thread, then glue them to the collage as desired. Reinsert the frame backing.

STEP 9 Apply gel medium to the back of the matchbox cookbook and glue it to the inside of the frame in the bottom left corner. Glue the rickrack trim around the front of the frame, as shown, and trim away the excess. Glue heart and cherry buttons to the top left, bottom left and bottom right corners.

STEP 10

Glue the mini utensils to the top right corner of the frame. I used a mini potholder and rolling pin here, but you can also find cute mini spoons like the ones on page 44 at your local craft store.

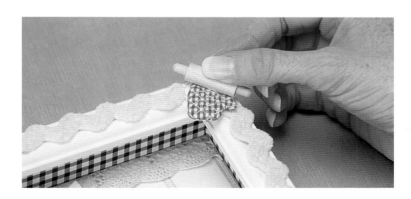

STEP 11

Stand the frame upright and glue the milk bottles along the bottom edge. Add game tiles spelling the word "cake" to the top of the frame.

DANCING CHEEK TO CHEEK

ROMANCE IS A WONDERFUL THING.

It can overwhelm us and color everything in our world. In the movie *Romancing the Stone*, Kathleen Turner's character (a romance novelist) says that she is not a hope*less*, but a hope*ful*, romantic. I like the distinction. Hope*less* implies a passive, almost defeatist attitude that is never really fulfilled. But hope*ful*? That, to me, is a wonderful way to approach life. To be hopeful allows me to look for and expect the best, even if it takes a while to arrive.

I've always loved romantic stories; ones in which two strong people meet, maybe clash, create sparks and find a way to keep that flame alive without burning up. That's where the real story takes shape. Not the dramatic beginning of the tale, but the part that comes after the final kiss dissolves into "The End." I've always believed that true love stories never end. "Happily ever after" is really just the beginning of the adventure.

Lucky me, I've enjoyed a staggeringly happy marriage. After fifteen years, Charlie and I are muddling contentedly through and having a ball. Part of our secret is to focus on what we love about one another, rather than how we make each other crazy. Victor Hugo once said, *"The supreme happiness in life is the conviction that we are loved."* Make the projects in this chapter and remind your own beloved of how much you care.

EVER AFTER

ever after

WHEN I WAS MAKING THIS CARD, I imagined a story in which a couple met, exchanged letters, fell in love and shared a life together. Perhaps they even passed their story and letters along to their children's children. Imagine making this card using copies of old family photos to tell a real-life story for succeeding generations. As you create, think about how the elements of your design support the story you are telling. For instance, to represent two lives becoming one, I bound the frames together with wire and dangled a heart charm between them.

"Love sought is good, but giv'n unsought is better."

WILLIAM SHAKESPEARE

MATERIALS FOR SIDE-FOLD CARD

Card: ivory cardstock cut to
10" x 6½" (25.4cm x 16.5cm),
then folded to 5" x 6½"
(12.7cm x 16.5cm)

Red and cream print paper cut to
4¼" x 6¼" (10.8cm x 15.9cm)

Dark red paper cut to 4" x 5⅜"
(10.2cm x 13.7cm)

Red handmade paper cut to
3¼" x 2¾" (8.3cm x 7cm)

Love letters paper

Two small photos or color copies

Two tiny gold frames

One heart charm

Two small brads

7" (17.8cm) piece of
embroidered ribbon

6" (15.2cm) piece of twill tape

6" (15.2cm) piece of thin wire

Tiny alphabet stamps

Dark red chalk

Dark red and black pigment inks

Walnut Stain distress ink

Cutting, punching and scoring
tools (see page 122 for options)

Adhesives (see page 122 for
options)

RED AND CREAM PRINT PAPER
BY PSX • DARK RED PAPER BY
K&COMPANY • LOVE LETTERS
PAPER BY SARAH LUGG • PHOTOS
BY ARTCHIX STUDIO • TINY
GOLD FRAMES BY HIRSCHBERG
SCHUTZ & CO • TINY ALPHABET
STAMPS BY HERO ARTS • TWILL
TAPE BY WRIGHT'S • DISTRESS
INK BY RANGER

TIP: A COTTON SWAB
OR FOAM EYESHADOW
BRUSH WORKS GREAT FOR
APPLYING CHALK.

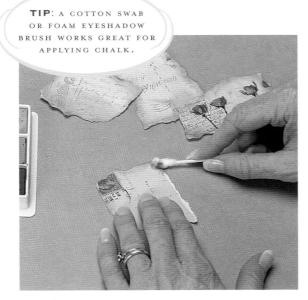

STEP 1 Tear out various images from the love letters paper and apply dark red chalk to the edges.

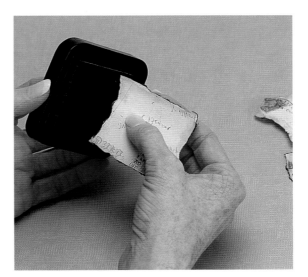

STEP 2 Drag the edges through Walnut Stain distress ink.

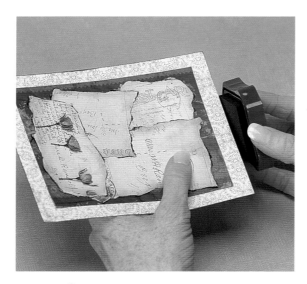

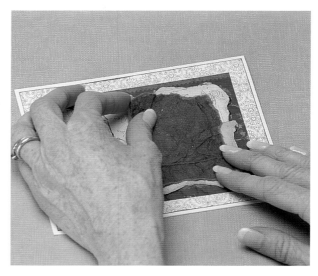

STEP 3 Glue the torn pieces from the love letters paper to the dark red paper, overlapping them to form a rectangle. Glue the dark red paper to the red and cream print paper and ink the edges with dark red pigment ink. Glue this layered piece to the front of the ivory card.

STEP 4 Tear the edges off the red handmade paper, pulling toward you as you tear so that the rough edges are exposed. Glue the torn paper to the card.

STEP 5 Remove the backs from the tiny gold frames. String the heart charm onto a piece of thin wire, then bind the frames together with the wire, as shown.

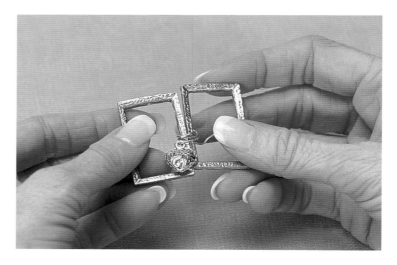

STEP 6 Insert the photos into the frames and trim away the excess.

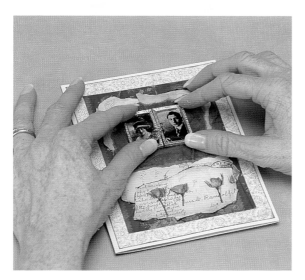

STEP **7** Use gel medium to attach the frames over the red handmade paper on the card.

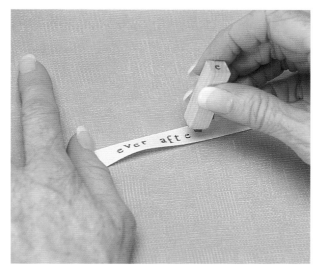

STEP **8** Use black pigment ink and tiny alphabet stamps to stamp the words "ever after" onto a piece of twill tape.

STEP **9**

Remove the wires from the embroidered ribbon. Lay the twill tape over the ribbon and make slits at each end through both pieces with a craft knife. Insert brads into the holes and bend the prongs outward to hold them in place. Trim the embroidered ribbon to about 6" (15.2cm).

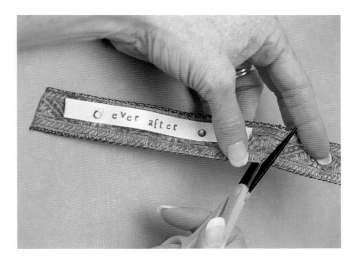

STEP **10**

Apply gel medium to the back of the ribbon and position it across the middle of the card.

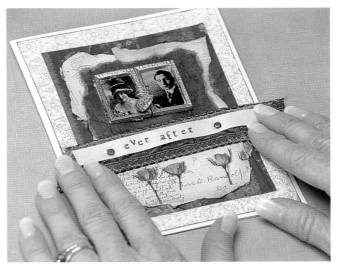

BE MINE, SWEET VALENTINE

ARE YOU OLD ENOUGH TO REMEMBER making valentines for your favorite people? The glue, the glitter, the paper doilies. You hardly ever see handmade valentines these days. This card incorporates the classic phrase "Be Mine" and the color red, along with a red rose, which is the traditional symbol for love. The envelope is created by tracing and cutting out a template by a company called Hot Off the Press. It can hold a romantic message inside. The French newsprint paper and walnut ink "aging" technique give this card a vintage feel. However, with the bottle cap and beaded wire ticket, it is definitely not your grandmother's valentine. To reduce bulk for mailing, feel free to smash the bottle cap with a hammer before inserting the letter sticker.

"To love deeply in one direction makes us more loving in all others."

ANNE-SOPHIE SWETCHINE

MATERIALS FOR TOP-FOLD CARD

Card: red cardstock cut to 7" x 10" (17.8cm x 25.4cm), then folded to 7" x 5" (12.7cm x 12.7cm)

Black text print paper cut to 6¾" x 3⅜" (17.2cm x 8.6cm)

Floral print paper cut to 6¾" x 4⅛" (17.2cm x 10.5cm)

Two strips of French newsprint paper cut to 6¾" x 1½ (17.2cm x 3.8cm)

Red diamond print paper torn to 3" x 1½ (7.6cm x 3.8cm)

Buff paper

Scraps of lace print and crackle paper

Small envelope template

Two small price tags with strings

One old ticket stub

Typewriter key, letter and clear dimensional stickers

One old bottle cap

One silk rosebud

Red beads

6¾" (17.2cm) piece of ivory crochet trim

Two 6¾" (17.2cm) pieces and one 3" (7.6cm) piece of black checked ribbon

12" (30.5cm) piece of thin wire

Tiny alphabet stamps

Black pigment ink

Walnut ink in small bowl

Antique Linen distress ink

Cutting, punching and scoring tools (see page 122 for options)

Adhesives (see page 122 for options)

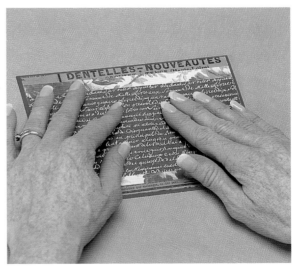

BLACK TEXT AND FRENCH NEWSPRINT PAPERS BY 7GYPSIES • FLORAL PRINT PAPER BY ANNA GRIFFIN, INC • RED DIAMOND PRINT PAPER BY K&COMPANY • LACE PRINT PAPER BY KAREN FOSTER DESIGN • CRACKLE PAPER BY DEBBIE MUMM • SMALL ENVELOPE TEMPLATE BY HOT OFF THE PRESS • TAGS BY AVERY • STICKERS BY COLORBÖK (FLAVIA COLLECTION) AND EK SUCCESS • TINY ALPHABET STAMPS BY HERO ARTS • DISTRESS INK BY RANGER

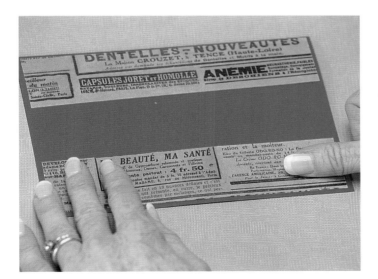

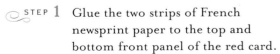

STEP 1 Glue the two strips of French newsprint paper to the top and bottom front panel of the red card.

STEP 2 Glue the floral print paper over the French newsprint paper, then the black text paper over the floral print paper, both centered on the card from top to bottom.

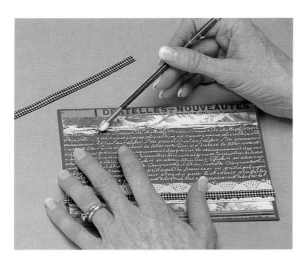

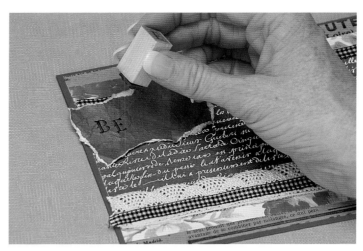

STEP 3 Use gel medium to glue the ivory crochet trim to the bottom of the black text print paper. Glue one of the 6³/₄" (17.2cm) black checked ribbons over the crochet trim and the other at the top of the black text print paper.

STEP 4 Distress the red diamond print paper as described on page 125, then glue it to the top left corner of the card. Use black pigment ink and tiny alphabet stamps to stamp the word "be" onto the paper.

STEP 5

Remove the strings from two small price tags. Using tweezers to hold the tags, dip them in a small bowl of walnut ink, or spray the ink onto the tags with a spray bottle. Shake off the excess, then pat the tags dry with a paper towel. Ink the strings or a 2" (5.1cm) piece of white thread as well, then allow to dry completely.

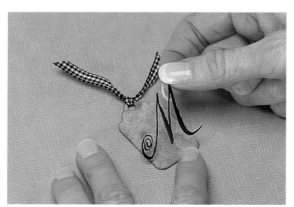

STEP 6 Tie the 3" (7.6cm) piece of black checked ribbon through the hole at the top of one of the small price tags and apply a letter "M" sticker.

STEP 7 Apply the letter "I" typewriter key sticker to a scrap of lace print paper. Layer a clear dimensional sticker over the letter and cut around it. Glue the letter to the inside of a bottle cap with gel medium.

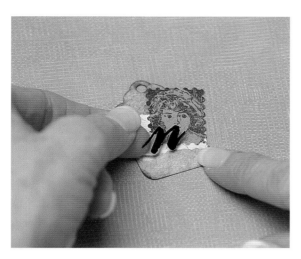

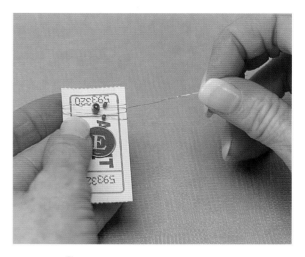

⌒STEP **8** Tear a 1" x 1" (2.5cm x 2.5cm) strip from a scrap of crackle paper, glue it to the other price tag and trim away the excess. Cut out a face from the leftover French newsprint paper and glue it over the crackle paper. Apply a letter "N" sticker next to the face, then tie the dyed string from step 5 back onto the tag.

⌒STEP **9** Glue a letter "E" typewriter key sticker to the ticket stub. Use double-sided tape to fasten one end of the wire to the back of the stub, then wrap the wire around once. String a red bead onto the wire, then wrap it around again. Repeat this a few more times, until you have four or five beaded wraps.

⌒STEP **10**

Align the letter components from steps 6–9 on the card to spell the word "mine" and attach with gel medium.

⌒STEP **11**

Trace the envelope template onto the back of the buff paper. Cut out the envelope, score and fold along the lines indicated by the template. (For instructions on scoring, see page 124.) Write a message inside the envelope and seal the flap closed with a glue stick.

⌒STEP **12**

Attach the silk rosebud over the envelope flap with gel medium, then glue the envelope to the front of the card.

TIMELESS LOVE

I MADE THIS CARD FOR MY PARENTS' forty-fifth wedding anniversary. That's my mom and dad on one of their first dates—a fraternity dinner dance in 1956. Mom even remembers the color of her dress: "a sort of deep rose color." After nearly half a century together, Robert and Arlene are still passionately in love and devoted to one another. Is it any wonder that I turned out to be a romantic at heart? The idea for the background came from the vintage patchwork paper. I adapted it to my color scheme and theme by cutting some of its panels out and making others from different patterned papers, and then reassembling them.

"To love and be loved is to feel the sun from both sides."

DAVID VISCOTT

MATERIALS FOR SIDE-FOLD CARD

Card: black cardstock cut to 12" x 6" (30.5cm x 15.2cm), then folded to 6" x 6" (15.2cm x 15.2cm)

Black cardstock cut to 4" x 4¼" (10.2cm x 10.8cm)

Polka dot paper cut to 2" x 3" (5.1cm x 7.6cm)

Floral print paper cut to 2" x 3" (5.1cm x 7.6cm)

Map print paper cut to 2" x 3" (5.1cm x 7.6cm)

French ledger paper cut to 2" x 3" (5.1cm x 7.6cm)

Music print paper cut to 2" x 3" (5.1cm x 7.6cm)

Diamond print paper cut to 2" x 3" (5.1cm x 7.6cm)

Scraps of vintage patchwork and white papers

Color copy of vintage photo cut to 3⅛" x 2⅝" (7.9cm x 6.7cm)

Clock face and hands stickers

One ball chain

Three photo anchors

Heart, lock and key charms

Three tiny black brads

One large eyelet

Label maker and label tape

Scrap of red ribbon

Tiny alphabet stamps

Pink and black pigment inks

Antique Linen distress ink

Eyelet setter and hammer

Cutting, punching and scoring tools (see page 122 for options)

Adhesives (see page 122 for options)

POLKA DOT PAPER BY DAISY D'S ◆ FLORAL PRINT PAPER BY RUSTY PICKLE ◆ MAP PRINT PAPER BY STICKER STUDIO ◆ FRENCH LEDGER PAPER BY 7GYPSIES ◆ VINTAGE PATCHWORK, MUSIC AND DIAMOND PRINT PAPERS BY LI'L DAVIS DESIGNS (VINTAGE PATCHWORK COLLECTION) ◆ CLOCK FACE AND HANDS STICKERS BY EK SUCCESS ◆ PHOTO ANCHORS BY MAKING MEMORIES ◆ CHARMS BY HIRSCHBERG SCHUTZ AND CO ◆ TINY ALPHABET STAMPS BY HERO ARTS ◆ LABEL MAKER AND TAPE BY DYMO ◆ DISTRESS INK BY RANGER

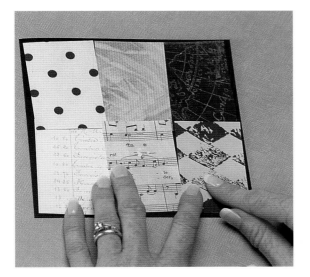

STEP 1 Arrange and glue all six of the 2" x 3" (5.1cm x 7.6cm) pieces of paper onto the front of the black card, as shown.

STEP 2 Attach the clock face and hands stickers over the map print paper with gel medium.

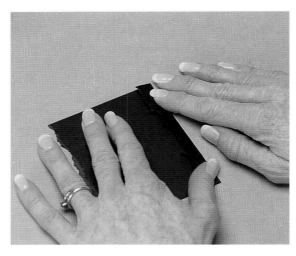

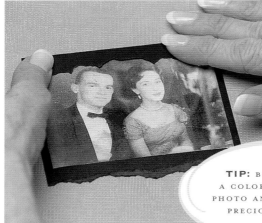

STEP 3 Swipe Antique Linen distress ink over the photo and smudge the edges with pink pigment ink.

STEP 4 Tear off and discard the top and bottom of the smaller piece of black cardstock. Score and fold it ¹/₂" (1.3cm) from the top, as described on page 124.

STEP 5

Glue the copy of the photo to the black cardstock, with the top edge of the photo up against the fold of the cardstock. Fold the flap over the top of the photo and glue in place.

TIP: BE SURE TO USE A COLOR COPY OF YOUR PHOTO AND PRESERVE THE PRECIOUS ORIGINAL.

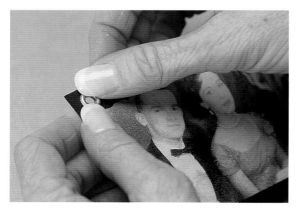

STEP 6 Punch a hole in the top left corner of the folded flap and set a large fabric eyelet in the hole. (For instructions, see page 124.)

STEP 7 Attach the black cardstock component to the card, roughly centered and on the diagonal, with double-sided tape.

STEP **8** Use an awl or sharp tool to pierce holes through the front panel of the card where you want your photo anchors. Place the anchors over the holes and insert brads through the anchors and the card. Bend the prongs outward to secure.

STEP **9** Use black pigment ink and tiny alphabet stamps to stamp the phrase "heart and soul" onto a scrap of vintage patchwork paper. Tear out around the letters and glue to the front of the card below the photo.

STEP **10** String two charms onto the ball chain and tie one to a piece of red ribbon. Attach the ball chain and ribbon to the card through the eyelet hole.

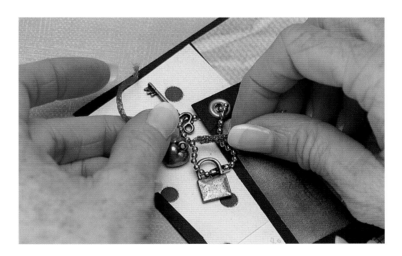

STEP **11** Using the label maker, spell out the phrase "timeless love." Peel the protective backing from the label tape and apply it to the card above the photo.

KISSES TO KEEP

I ADMIT TO ENJOYING EXTRAVAGANCE as much as the next girl; the bigger, the more over-the-top, the sparklier, the better! That being said, however, sometimes little things really are the best. Especially when the presentation is as gorgeous as this diminutive project that nestles in the palm of your hand. There is a certain delight in opening the successive layers to reveal the tiny treasures inside. It makes a sweet gift for someone you treasure. You can also adapt the box to hold a baby ring for a newborn, a charm bracelet for a young girl or even a love letter.

"A kiss is a lovely trick designed by nature to stop speech when words become superfluous."

INGRID BERGMAN

MATERIALS FOR BOX AND ENVELOPE

Red damask print paper

Red and cream print paper

Red text print paper cut to
2⅛" x 5" (5.4cm x 12.7cm)

Scraps of cream cardstock and red mulberry paper

Envelope template

One artisan label

One small matchbox

One silk rosebud

One tiny clear bottle

Tiny red glass beads

One poem stone

Gold stamped foil lace

20" (50.8cm) piece of ivory wired ribbon with gold trim

3" (7.6cm) piece of sheer white ribbon

Gold leafing pen

Antique Linen distress ink

Ivory acrylic paint

Cutting, punching and scoring tools (see page 122 for options)

Adhesives (see page 122 for options)

RED DAMASK PRINT PAPER, ENVELOPE TEMPLATE AND POEM STONE BY SONNETS STAMPS ◆ RED AND CREAM PRINT PAPER BY PSX ◆ RED TEXT PAPER AND TINY BOTTLE BY 7GYPSIES ◆ ARTISAN LABEL BY MAKING MEMORIES ◆ GOLD STAMPED FOIL LACE BY RUBBER BABY BUGGY BUMPERS ◆ DISTRESS INK BY RANGER

TIP: GEL MEDIUM HAS A TENDENCY TO BUCKLE PAPER, SO YOU WILL NEED TO BURNISH IT, OR RUB IT SMOOTH WITH A BONE FOLDER, TO GET OUT ALL THE WRINKLES AND BUBBLES.

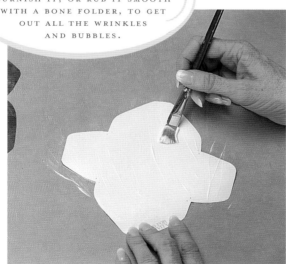

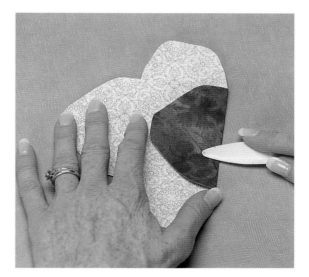

STEP 1 Trace the envelope template onto the backs of the red damask and red and cream print papers. Cut out both pieces and glue them back to back. Trim around the edges if necessary to make them symmetrical.

STEP 2 Score, fold and crease the flaps as indicated on the template. (For scoring instructions, see page 124.)

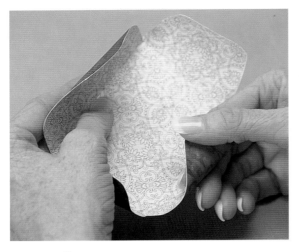

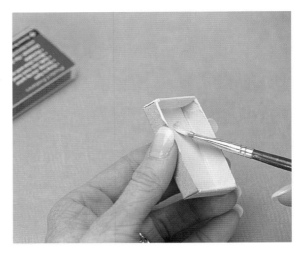

STEP **3** Use your finger to curl the flaps inward as the gel medium dries. This will give your envelope a "puffy" look. Trace around the edges with gold leafing pen. Set the envelope aside for use in step 11.

STEP **4** Paint the inside and outside of the matchbox drawer with ivory acrylic paint. Allow to dry.

STEP **5**

Coat the matchbox cover with gel medium, cover with red text paper and trim off the excess. Line the edges of the box with gold leafing pen.

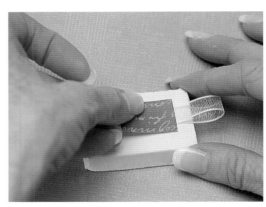

STEP **6** Fold a piece of sheer white ribbon to make a loop. Glue the ends of the ribbon onto the bottom of the matchbox drawer, then cover them with a tiny scrap of leftover red text paper. The ribbon becomes a pull tab.

STEP **7** Cut a scrap of red and cream print paper to 2" x 1¼" (5.1cm x 3.2cm) and glue it to the inside of the drawer to line it.

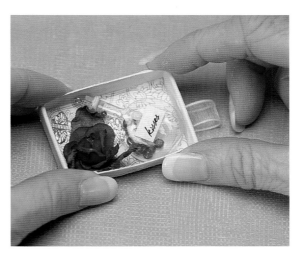

STEP **8** Print or write "kisses" on a scrap of cream cardstock and trim around the letters. Glue the word to the front of the tiny bottle with gel medium. Remove the cork from the bottle and fill it with tiny red glass beads. Secure the cork back in place with a drop of gel medium.

STEP **9** Glue a piece of gold stamped foil, the tiny bottle and a silk rosebud to the inside of the matchbox drawer with gel medium.

STEP **10**

Tear a small piece of mulberry paper and fluff the edges. Glue the mulberry paper to the top of the matchbox cover, then glue a poem stone over the mulberry paper. Slip the drawer inside the cover.

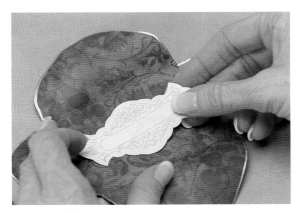

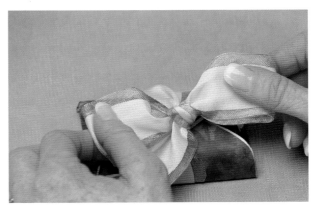

STEP **11** Swipe the artisan label with Antique Linen distress ink, then glue the label to the outside center panel of the envelope.

STEP **12** Position the matchbox inside the envelope, fold in the flaps and tie a decorative bow around the envelope with ivory and gold wired ribbon.

JOURNEYS OF THE HEART AND SOUL

MANY OF MY OWN TRAVEL FANTASIES WERE formed by reading about the "Golden Age" of travel—the time of the Grand Tour, steamer trunks, luxury trains and elegant travel costumes. I really don't mind that this reality doesn't exist anymore, or that, for most people, it never did. What does captivate me is the sense of occasion and importance that surrounded a journey.

You may love to travel, dream of traveling or simply view life itself as a great journey. I love the idea of exploration, the notion that any adventure may lead to discoveries. Whether it's a new restaurant, a new experience or a new way of seeing myself, I want to live it all.

To me, that's the beauty of life. There are lessons to be learned, wisdom to discover, strangers who may become friends, and we can't know any of it in advance. But we've got to go *somewhere* to find out. The trick, I think, is not to drag our tiresome old outlook along with us. Better to approach each journey with a willingness to see things anew than to miss the good stuff through lack of attention.

The projects in this chapter reflect some of my own admittedly romanticized notions of journeys. Use them as a jumping-off point in your own creative journeying.

A DAY AT THE BEACH

THE STRIPES AND COLORS IN THIS CARD remind me of beach balls, umbrellas and those marvelous old-fashioned bathing suits. In my mind, I picture a timeworn seaside village; perhaps a place one visits every year. In this place, the smell of the sea mingles with the scents of sunscreen and taffy, creating an irresistible perfume. I wanted to capture the salt air, the sand—the look of things weathered by the years. For me, this nostalgic place exists only in my mind, as the ghost of days I've only dreamed of. Maybe yours is real.

"One cannot collect all the beautiful shells on the beach. One can collect only a few, and they are more beautiful if they are few."

ANNE MORROW LINDBERGH

MATERIALS FOR TOP-FOLD CARD

Card: oatmeal cardstock cut to 9¹⁄₈" x 8¹⁄₂" (23.2cm x 21.6cm), then folded to 9¹⁄₈" x 4¹⁄₄" (23.2cm x 10.8cm)

Striped paper cut to 4¹⁄₄" x 3¹⁄₂" (10.8cm x 8.9cm)

Blue paper cut to 4¹⁄₈" x 9" (10.5cm x 22.9cm)

Red paper cut to 2" x 2³⁄₄" (5.1cm x 7cm)

Map print paper cut to 1³⁄₈" x 2³⁄₄" (3.5cm x 7cm)

Alphabet print paper

Dictionary travel print paper with "beach" definition

Scrap of red text print paper

One small price tag and one medium shipping tag

Letter "B" stencil

Typewriter key and letter stickers

Metal letter "C" charm

Three small eyelets

One watch crystal

One small starfish

Fishing net or cheesecloth

15" (38CM) of hemp cord

Walnut ink in spray bottle

Cream, burnt umber and black acrylic paint

Eyelet setter and hammer

Cutting, punching and scoring tools (see page 122 for options)

Adhesives (see page 122 for options)

STRIPED PAPER BY TREEHOUSE DESIGNS ◆ BLUE AND DICTIONARY TRAVEL PRINT PAPERS BY PEBBLES, INC (REAL LIFE COLLECTION) ◆ RED PAPER BY THE PAPER LOFT ◆ MAP PAPER BY SCENIC ROUTE PAPER CO ◆ ALPHABET PAPER BY 7GYPSIES ◆ RED TEXT PRINT PAPER BY K&COMPANY (LIFE'S JOURNEY COLLECTION) ◆ TAGS BY AVERY ◆ LETTER STENCILS BY HEADLINE (2" GOTHIC CAPS, NUMBERS AND SYMBOLS) ◆ STICKERS BY EK SUCCESS AND CREATIVE IMAGINATIONS ◆ METAL CHARM AND EYELETS BY MAKING MEMORIES ◆ WATCH CRYSTAL BY SCRAPWORKS (FRAMES AND HUGZ COLLECTION)

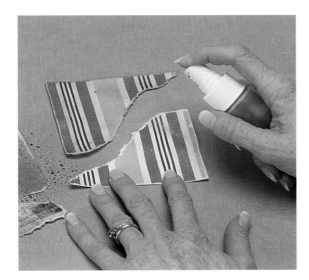

◦STEP 1 Tear the striped paper in half diagonally, then tear out the "beach" definition from the travel paper. Distress the striped and blue papers and the definition as described on page 125, then spritz with walnut ink and allow to dry.

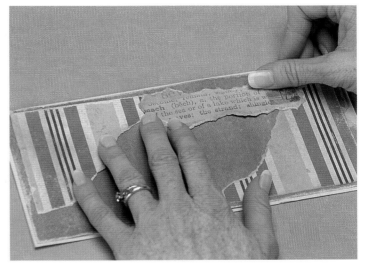

◦STEP 2 When the pieces are dry, glue them to the front of the oatmeal card as shown.

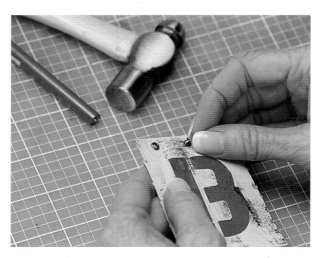

STEP 3 Drybrush the letter "B" stencil with burnt umber acrylic paint, allow to dry, then drybrush again with cream acrylic paint. For quick drying, use a heat embossing tool.

STEP 4 Distress a piece of red paper and glue the stencil over it so that the red paper shows through. Punch three holes in the top of the stencil and set small eyelets in each of the holes, as described on page 124.

STEP 5

Tear off a 2¹/₂" (38CM) wide strip of red text print paper. Spritz the strip and a small price tag with walnut ink and allow to dry. Then, apply glue to the back of the strip and wrap it around the tag.

STEP 6 Cut out the letter "A" from the alphabet print paper and glue it over the text paper on the price tag. Glue a scrap of red paper to the back of the tag and trim off the excess. Re-punch the hole in the tag if necessary.

STEP 7 Distress the metal "C" charm, then paint it with black acrylic paint and allow to dry.

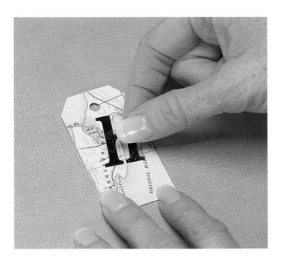

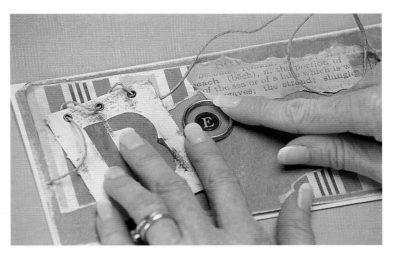

STEP 8 Glue the map print paper to the front of a shipping tag and trim away the excess. Re-punch the hole in the tag and apply a letter "H" sticker.

STEP 9 Thread hemp cord through the eyelets on the letter "B" stencil and glue the stencil to the front of the card. Apply the letter "E" typewriter key sticker next to the stencil, then position the watch crystal over the "E" sticker and press down on the crystal to make indentations with the prongs. Use a craft knife to make slits in the paper on the indentations, then reposition the watch crystal prongs through the slits.

STEP 10

String the hemp cord through the small "A" price tag and glue the tag to the card. Use gel medium to glue the cord down in various spots, bending and looping it in a random fashion as you go. String the metal "C" charm onto the cord and allow it to dangle.

STEP 11 String the "H" shipping tag onto the cord and glue it to the card. Trim the cord, leaving a 2" (5.1cm) tail.

TIP: IF YOU CAN'T FIND FISHING NET, USE CHEESECLOTH DYED WITH WALNUT INK INSTEAD.

STEP 12 Dab the fishing net and starfish with gel medium and attach them to the card, tucking part of the net under the dangling "C" charm.

THE BEST WAY TO TRAVEL

I LOVE THE IDEA THAT OUR JOURNEY THROUGH LIFE includes traveling companions. With them, we can explore and discover the world's delights, approach adventures with greater confidence, and more easily navigate bumps in the road. To lend a timeless note to this card, I used a fan print paper that made me think of the décor used in cruise ships long ago. I also think this ribbon is so luscious. It looks like it might have been collected on various trips and kept as a reminder of journeys taken. Mica, a natural mineral that can be separated into thin sheets and used as an overlay, is another favorite material of mine. It is easy to work with, looks both earthy and vintage, and seems somewhat exotic. Mica tiles are transparent and thin enough to be cut with regular scissors.

"I travel not to go anywhere, but to go. I travel for travel's sake."

ROBERT LOUIS STEVENSON

MATERIALS FOR SIDE-FOLD CARD

Card: cream cardstock cut to 10" x 7" (25.4cm x 17.8cm), then folded to 5" x 7" (12.7cm x 17.8cm)

Dark brown cardstock cut to 3¹/₂" x 5¹/₂" (8.9cm x 14cm)

Fan print paper cut to 4³/₄" x 6³/₄" (12.1cm x 17.2cm)

Definitions print paper torn to 3³/₄" x 5¹/₂" (9.5cm x 14cm)

Antique leather print paper cut to 1³/₄" x 3¹/₄" (4.5cm x 8.3cm)

Vintage travel images

Decorative labels

One piece of mica

One circle clip

Two photo anchors

Two copper brads

Several 12"–14" (30.5cm–35.6cm) pieces of decorative fiber

Decorative stamp

Turquoise pigment ink

Antique Linen distress ink

Cutting, punching and scoring tools (see page 122 for options)

Adhesives (see page 122 for options)

FAN PRINT PAPER BY FRANCES MEYER ◆ DEFINITIONS PRINT PAPER BY CAROLEE'S CREATIONS (REMEMBER THE DAY COLLECTION) ◆ ANTIQUE LEATHER PRINT PAPER BY KAREN FOSTER DESIGN ◆ VINTAGE TRAVEL IMAGES BY OUTDOORS AND MORE (VINTAGE PRESS COLLECTION) ◆ LABELS BY 7GYPSIES (LIBRARIE LABELS COLLECTION) ◆ MICA BY USARTQUEST ◆ PHOTO ANCHORS BY MAKING MEMORIES ◆ FIBERS BY SPECIAL EFFECTS (SEA BREEZE COLLECTION) ◆ DISTRESS INK BY RANGER

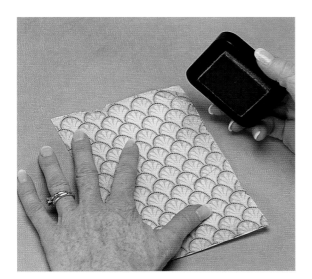

STEP 1 Swipe the fan print paper with Antique Linen distress ink to add an aged look. Continue distressing as desired.

STEP 2 Apply turquoise pigment ink to the decorative stamp (I used a vine stamp) and stamp onto the edges of the dark brown cardstock. Ink the edges, as well.

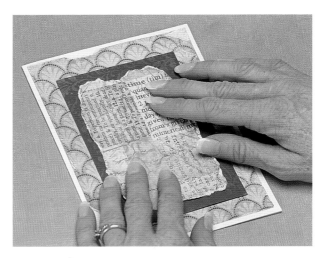

STEP **3** Glue the fan print paper to the front of the cream card, then glue all but the top left corner of the dark brown stamped cardstock to the fan print paper, centered in all directions.

STEP **4** Distress the definitions print paper, then crumple and uncrumple it a few times. Layer the uncrumpled paper over the dark brown cardstock and glue it down in a few areas, making sure some of the wrinkles are not attached.

STEP **5**

Cut out a vintage travel image and glue it to the antique leather print paper. Glue this layered piece over the definitions print paper, positioning it on a slight diagonal.

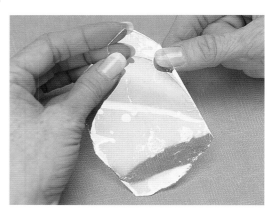

STEP **6** Insert your fingernail or a craft knife into the edge of the mica. It will split into layers easily. Gently peel the layers apart.

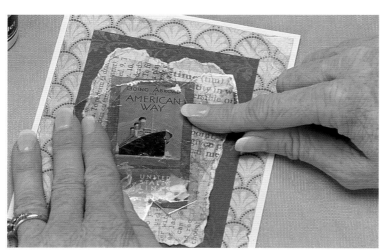

STEP **7** Glue thin layers of mica over the vintage travel image with Diamond Glaze.

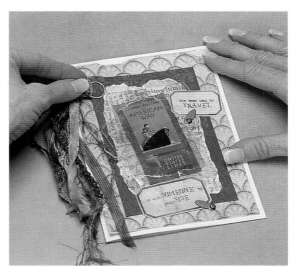

STEP 8 Print or write, "The best way to travel," on one label and, "is with someone by your side," on the other. Glue the labels above and below the vintage travel image. Cut a tiny slit in the front panel of the card below each label. Position the photo anchors over the slits, insert brads through the photo anchors and slits, and bend the prongs outward to secure.

STEP 9 Tie the fibers around a circle clip, then fasten the clip to the top left corner of the dark brown cardstock. Arrange the fibers decoratively.

FLOWER SILHOUETTE

Mica is wonderfully versatile material. For this card, I stamped a flower stem onto the mica and embossed it as described on page 34, steps 3 and 4. As you can see, the basic layout of the card remains the same, yet the mood changes completely when you use different colors and images. Yes, you have permission to experiment!

ETERNAL ITALY

A ROOM WITH A VIEW. THE ENCHANTED APRIL.

These novels-turned-movies were the inspiration for this
card. Writers, poets and composers have extolled the beauty
and charm Italy. Once I found this paper with the Italian
image on it, I started thinking about sipping wine in Venice,
savoring the art and architecture of Florence and basking in
the splendor of Rome. Everything came together; another
flight of fancy completed!

*"You may have
the universe if I
may have Italy."*

GUISEPPE VERDI

MATERIALS FOR TOP-FOLD CARD

Card: eggplant cardstock cut to 6" x 12" (15.2cm x 30.5cm), then folded to 6" x 6" (15.2cm x 15.2cm)

Medium purple cardstock cut to 3½" x 4½" (8.9cm x 11.4cm)

Purple marbled paper cut to 4⅞" x 5¾" (12.4cm x 14.6cm)

Purple script paper cut to 3⅝" x 6" (9.2cm x 15.2cm)

Italian print paper cut to 4½" x 4½" (11.4cm x 11.4cm)

Lavender mulberry paper cut to 2½" x 2" (6.4cm x 5.1cm)

Clear acetate

Grapes and faux postage stickers

Five large copper eyelets

8" (20.3cm) piece of copper tape

Three 6" (15.2cm) pieces of fiber

Column and Tower of Pisa stamps

Amethyst Pearlustre embossing powder

Deep plum and chestnut brown pigment inks

Antique Linen distress ink

Walnut ink in a spray bottle

Copper antiquing solution

Eyelet setter and hammer

Cutting, punching and scoring tools (see page 122 for options)

Adhesives (see page 122 for options)

PURPLE MARBLED PAPER BY COLORBÖK • PURPLE SCRIPT PAPER BY NRN DESIGNS • ITALIAN PRINT PAPER BY AUTUMN LEAVES • STICKERS BY LEISURE ARTS AND EK SUCCESS • COPPER EYELETS BY PRYM-DRITZ CORPORATION • FIBERS BY SPECIAL EFFECTS (SPRING COLLECTION) • COLUMN STAMP BY A STAMP IN THE HAND CO • TOWER OF PISA STAMP BY STAMPINGTON & COMPANY • EMBOSSING POWDER BY STAMPENDOUS! • DISTRESS INK BY RANGER • COPPER ANTIQUING SOLUTION BY MODERN OPTIONS

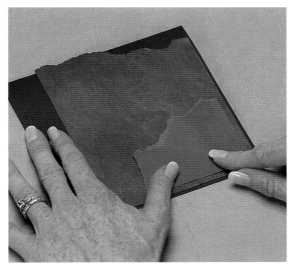

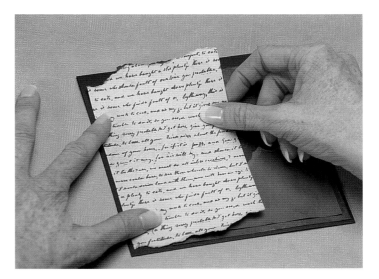

STEP 1 Tear off and discard the top ½" (1.3m) of the purple marbled paper and ink the edges of the remaining paper with deep plum pigment ink. Glue it to the front of the eggplant card, allowing the torn edge to stick up over the top. Spritz the medium purple cardstock with walnut ink, tear off and discard the top left corner and glue the rest to the bottom right corner of the purple marbled paper.

STEP 2 Tear off and discard the top and bottom off the purple script paper. Swipe the remaining paper with Antique Linen distress ink and glue it to the left side of the card over the other layers.

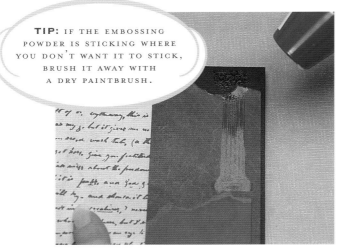

STEP **3** Ink the column stamp with deep plum pigment ink and stamp onto the top right corner of the purple marbled paper. Emboss the stamped image as described on page 34, steps 3 and 4.

STEP **4** Tear off the upper left and right corners of the Italian print paper. Ink the edges with chestnut brown pigment ink, then swipe the surface with Antique Linen distress ink. Set aside to dry.

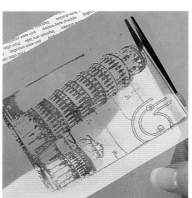

STEP **5**

Ink the Tower of Pisa stamp with chestnut brown pigment ink and stamp it onto a piece of clear acetate. Emboss the stamped image and trim around the edges.

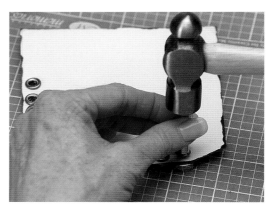

STEP **6** Attach the Tower of Pisa image to the Italian print paper with Diamond Glaze. Use the anywhere punch to make three holes down the left side and two holes in the upper right corner of the Italian print paper. Set large copper eyelets in each of the holes. (For instructions, see page 124.)

STEP **7** Tie one fiber through each of the three side eyelets and trim off the excess.

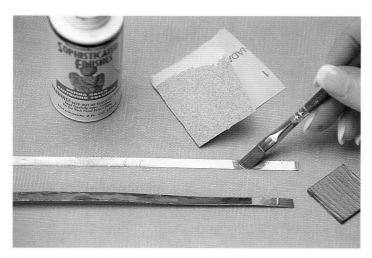

STEP 8 Lightly sand the copper tape with fine-grit sandpaper. Following the package instructions, brush the tape with copper antiquing solution and set it aside to carry on its chemical process. In a few hours, you should see a pretty patina. Patina is the greenish color that results from the corrosion of the copper.

STEP 9 Glue the Italian print paper from step 7 to the front of the card, centered in all directions. Position the antiqued copper tape across the bottom of the card and trim off the excess tape.

STEP 10

Distress the grape sticker and apply it over the copper tape in the bottom left corner of the card. Spritz the lavender mulberry paper with walnut ink, allow it to dry, then glue it to the bottom right corner of the card. Tear off and discard the bottom of the faux postage sticker. Ink along the tear of the remaining sticker with chestnut brown pigment ink and apply it over the mulberry paper.

LEAF EXHIBIT

Aged copper accents are so pretty. And a copper plant tag makes a cool label for an autumn leaf. To make the leaf panel and the text background paper, I painted, inked and sponged watercolor paper and a page from a second-hand book. Stamp the leaf with black solvent ink and smudge the edges with copper metallic rub-ons. To finish, edge the yellow-green panel with a copper leafing pen.

PARIS DREAMS

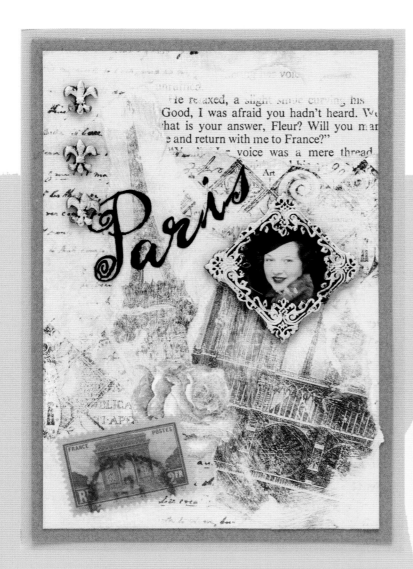

THE EIFFEL TOWER IS ONE OF THE COOLEST-LOOKING

structures I know of. I've not yet made it to visit Paris, so for now, I'll have to dream. A while back, I found an old book that I planned to alter. But before I cut, glued and painted it into unrecognizability, I just couldn't help browsing through it. Turns out it was an old Harlequin romance about a moody Frenchman and the sweet English nurse who falls in love with him. Fabulous, corny, irresistible. The card uses text from the book to tell a little story of its own.

"...for all of Paris is a moveable feast."

Ernest Hemingway

MATERIALS FOR SIDE-FOLD CARD

Card: light blue cardstock cut to 10" x 7" (25.4cm x 17.8cm), then folded to 5" x 7" (12.7cm x 17.8cm)

Medium blue cardstock cut to 4³/₄" x 6³/₄" (12.1cm x 17.2cm)

Watercolor paper cut to 4¹/₂" x 6¹/₂" (11.4cm x 16.5cm)

Roses montage paper

Scrap of white paper

Page from an old book

Vintage Paris postcards

Color copy of vintage photo cut to 1¹/₂" x 1¹/₂" (3.8cm x 3.8cm)

Letter and vintage postage stickers 1¹/₂" x 1¹/₂" (3.8cm x 3.8cm)

metal frame

Three fleur de lis embellishments

Script and diamond collage stamps

Light blue pigment ink

Black permanent ink

Antique Linen distress ink

Cream acrylic paint

Cutting, punching and scoring tools (see page 122 for options)

Adhesives (see page 122 for options)

ROSES MONTAGE PAPER BY PSX ◆ VINTAGE PARIS POSTCARDS BY PROVO CRAFT (ALTERED ELEMENTS COLLAGE PACK) ◆ STICKERS BY COLORBÖK AND ME AND MY BIG IDEAS ◆ METAL FRAME AND FLEUR DE LIS EMBELLISHMENT BY THE CARD CONNECTION ◆ SCRIPT STAMP BY INKADINKADO ◆ DIAMOND COLLAGE STAMP BY STAMPERS ANONYMOUS ◆ DISTRESS INK BY RANGER

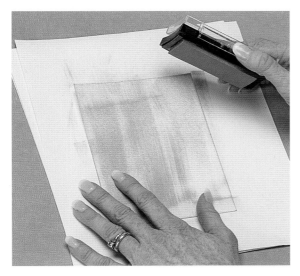

STEP 1 Swipe the watercolor paper with light blue pigment ink and allow to dry.

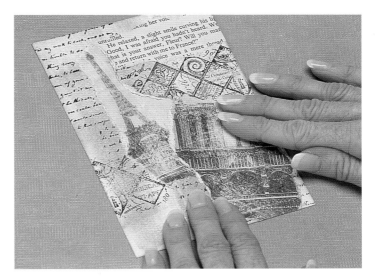

STEP 2 Ink the diamond collage and script stamps with black permanent ink and randomly stamp onto the watercolor paper. Tear out a few images from the vintage postcards and a block of text from an old book. Distress them with sandpaper and Antique Linen distress ink, then glue them onto the watercolor paper.

STEP 3 Use a foam brush, sponge or crumpled paper towel to dab cream acrylic paint onto the edges and along the seams of the images on the watercolor paper. Allow to dry.

STEP 4 Glue the metal frame over the vintage photo and trim away the excess. Glue the frame to the watercolor paper, then smudge the frame with cream acrylic paint. Dab off the excess paint with a paper towel.

STEP 5 Apply letter stickers to spell the word "Paris" across the watercolor paper.

STEP 6 Cut out a rose from the rose montage paper and glue it to the bottom center of the watercolor paper collage. Apply the vintage postage sticker to the bottom left corner of the collage, overlapping the rose.

STEP 7 Glue the medium blue cardstock to the light blue card, then glue the watercolor paper collage to the medium blue cardstock.

82

ﾠSTEP **8** Attach three fleur de lis embellishments down the top left side of the watercolor paper with gel medium.

ﾠSTEP **9** Apply cream acrylic paint to the fleur de lis embellishments and dab off the excess with a paper towel. Allow to dry.

PAGES IN HISTORY

Making a bookmark can be less intimidating and time-consuming than making a card. Just line up a bunch of papers and try different color combinations and decorative elements. Then, punch a hole in the top and tie some decorative fibers through the hole. You can also laminate the bookmark for extra durability.

THE WORLD OUTSIDE YOUR WINDOW

AS MUCH AS I LOVE TO TRAVEL AND SEE new things, I'm also a homebody. No matter how far I wander, I'm always eager to get back to my own nest. There's nothing quite so satisfying as the little surprises that can pop up in familiar surroundings. I find a great deal of pleasure right in my own back yard—literally!

The house I live in is new, so the garden was truly designed from the ground up. The design process involved in creating an extensive perennial garden was so much fun. On paper, I was able to play with color, form, texture and bloom time. Even though the garden is off to a good start, it is still a work in progress. During my planning, I ran across a verse by George Eliot that really spoke to me: "*You love the roses—so do I. I wish the sky would rain down roses.*" To try to accomplish that, I'm continually adding new plants to my garden, especially roses. It seems a worthy goal to wedge as many vintage and shrub roses as possible into this suburban lot.

The projects in this chapter reflect my love of gardening, color and texture. I've also incorporated a cottage-chic look, which seems to work well with the gardening theme. Look outside your window and be inspired by what you see there.

LET THE SUN SHINE IN

"In this house, there is a constant succession of small events."

JANE AUSTEN

I GREW UP IN SOUTHERN CALIFORNIA, so I never really experienced the harshness of winter until I moved to Ohio. After fifteen years, I'm still thrilled by the change of the seasons. Each year, there are things to look forward to. For instance, there comes a day in spring when you can finally open the windows and let in the fresh air and light. Everything seems new and awake and alive. I tried to capture a bit of that feeling in this card. The fresh pink and green color scheme is a favorite of mine, and the rolled paper hints at a window treatment.

MATERIALS FOR SIDE-FOLD CARD

Card: light green cardstock cut to 10" x 7" (25.4cm x 17.8cm), then folded to 5" x 7" (12.7cm x 17.8cm)

Gingham paper cut to 4⁷⁄₈" x 6⁷⁄₈"(12.4cm x 17.8cm)

Pink floral print paper cut to 2¹⁄₂" x 5" (6.4cm x 12.7cm)

Bird print paper cut to 4⁷⁄₈" x 4" (12.4cm x 10.2cm)

Ruler print paper

Ribbed green vellum

Floral-themed ephemera

One silk rosebud

Two 12" (30.5cm) pieces of light green satin ribbon

7" (17.8cm) piece of crochet trim

Decorative buttons threaded with embroidery floss

Vintage Photo distress ink

Cutting, punching and scoring tools (see page 122 for options)

Adhesives (see page 122 for options)

PINK FLORAL, BIRD PRINT AND GINGHAM PAPERS BY COLORBÖK (TRACY PORTER COLLECTION) ♦ RULER PRINT PAPER BY 7GYPSIES ♦ FLORAL-THEMED EPHEMERA BY PROVO CRAFT (ALTERED ELEMENTS COLLECTION) ♦ DISTRESS INK BY RANGER

STEP 1 Glue the gingham paper to the front panel of the light green card.

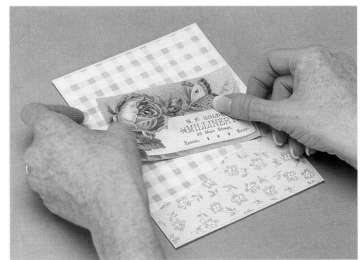

STEP 2 Tear the top off the pink floral print paper and discard. Glue the remaining paper to the bottom of the card over the gingham paper. Glue a large floral image from the floral-themed ephemera to the center of the gingham paper, positioning it diagonally.

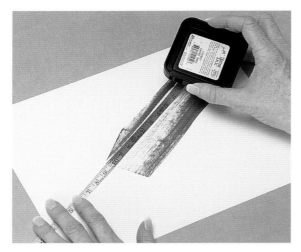

STEP **3** Cut one ruler strip off the ruler print paper. Ink the strip with Vintage Photo distress ink, then wipe away the excess with a paper towel.

STEP **4** Glue the ruler strip to the card vertically, about ½" (13cm) from the left side. Trim off the excess.

STEP **5**

Use a pencil to roll the long edge of the bird print paper to about 2" (5.1cm) from the top.

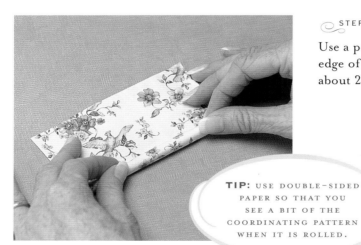

TIP: USE DOUBLE-SIDED PAPER SO THAT YOU SEE A BIT OF THE COORDINATING PATTERN WHEN IT IS ROLLED.

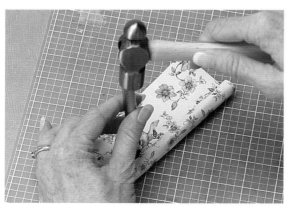

STEP **6** Measure and mark 1" (2.5cm) in from each side of the unrolled portion of the paper. Punch holes at the marks with an anywhere punch.

STEP **7** Thread pieces of light green satin ribbon through the holes and tie bows around the roll to hold it in place. Trim the ribbon ends at an angle.

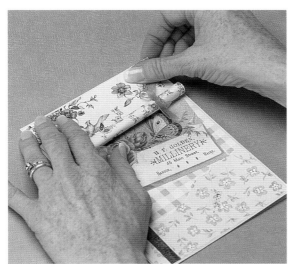

STEP 8 Apply gel medium to the back of the unrolled portion of the paper and glue it across the top of the card.

STEP 9 Glue another floral image to the ribbed green vellum and tear around the edges of the vellum. Glue the piece to the bottom left corner of the card.

STEP 10 Glue a piece of crochet trim across the top of the card with gel medium and cut off the edges of the trim, allowing them to hang over a bit.

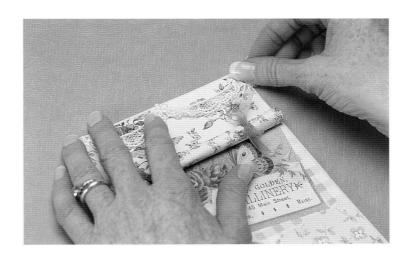

TIP: IF YOU CHOOSE A BUTTON WITH A SHANK ON THE BACK, CUT IT OFF WITH WIRE CUTTERS.

STEP 11 Attach two decorative buttons and a silk rosebud to the bottom right corner of the card with gel medium.

BLOSSOM BY BLOSSOM

CLOTHESLINES ARE RARELY SEEN ANYMORE, but the
idea of hanging things out to air dry still seems appealing. Here,
I've dangled three small spring-themed tags from a ribbon. If you
want to further emphasize the cottage-chic vibe, go ahead and sand,
crumple and rough up the paper elements as you assemble the card.
You can even give it a light whitewash with acrylic paint. Just for fun,
I've used "*printemps,*" the French word for spring, on the front of the
card, but feel free to change this to suit your mood.

> *"Blossom by blossom*
> *the spring begins."*
> SWINBURNE

MATERIALS FOR TOP-FOLD CARD

Card: light green cardstock cut to 7" x 10" (17.8cm x 5.4cm), then folded to 7" x 5" (17.8cm x 12.7cm)

Script paper cut to 6⁵/₈" x 4³/₄" (16.8cm x 12.1cm)

Green paisley paper cut to 5¹/₂" x 3⁵/₈" (14cm x 9.2cm)

Pink floral print paper cut to 5³/₄" x 3⁷/₈" (14.6cm x 9.8cm)

Bird print paper

Green gingham paper

Ribbed green vellum

Floral-themed ephemera

One metal rim circle tag, one metal rim rectangular vellum tag and one small price tag

Glass beads

Four silver brads

One silk rosebud

8" (20.3cm) pieces of pink and green braided ribbon and light green and light pink satin ribbon

12" (30.5cm) of pink and green blended ribbon

Decorative buttons

One headpin

Tiny alphabet stamps

Black pigment ink

Cutting, punching and scoring tools (see page 122 for options)

Adhesives (see page 122 for options)

SCRIPT PAPER BY 7GYPSIES • GREEN PAISLEY PAPER BY ANNA GRIFFIN, INC • PINK FLORAL, BIRD PRINT AND GING-HAM PAPERS BY COLORBÖK (TRACY PORTER COLLECTION) • FLORAL-THEMED EPHEMERA BY PROVO CRAFT (ALTERED ELE-MENTS COLLECTION) • TAGS BY AVERY AND MAKING MEMORIES • TINY ALPHABET STAMPS BY HERO ARTS

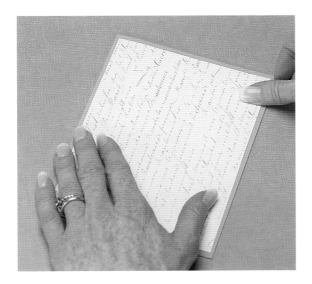

STEP 1 Glue the script paper to the front panel of the light green card.

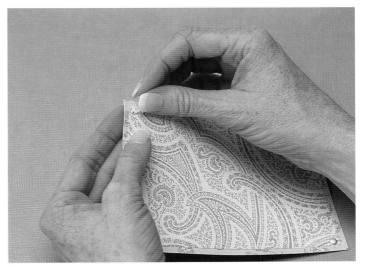

STEP 2 Layer the green paisley paper over the pink floral print paper. Pierce holes in all four corners of the paisley paper with an awl or thick needle. Insert brads into the holes and bend the prongs outward.

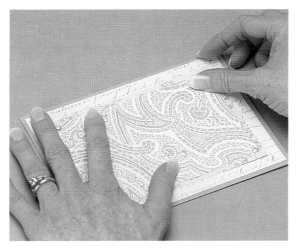

STEP **3** Glue the layered piece from step 2 to the card.

STEP **4** Glue a scrap of bird print paper over a small price tag and trim around the edges with a craft knife.

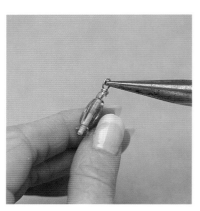

STEP **5**

To make a bead dangle, string a few decorative beads onto a headpin and use needle-nose pliers to twist the straight end of the headpin into a loop. Wrap the excess wire around the base of the loop.

STEP **6** String a piece of pink and green braided ribbon through the bead dangle loop, then tie the dangle onto the small price tag from step 4.

STEP **7** Cut out a 1¹/₂" (3.8cm) circle from a scrap of green gingham paper, then cut a small fairy from the floral-themed ephemera. Glue the gingham circle to the metal rim circle tag, then glue the fairy over the gingham circle. Re-punch the hole in the tag.

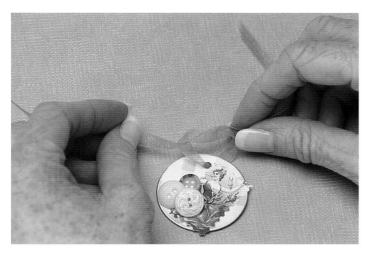

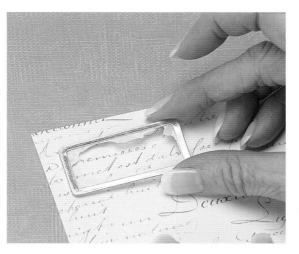

STEP **8** Glue decorative buttons to the circle tag with gel medium, cutting off the shanks if necessary, then tie a piece of green satin ribbon through the hole in the tag.

STEP **9** Tear the center out of the metal rim rectangular vellum tag. Apply gel medium around the metal edges on one side of the tag and glue it to a scrap of script paper. Allow the gel medium to dry, then trim around the edges. Re-punch the hole in the tag.

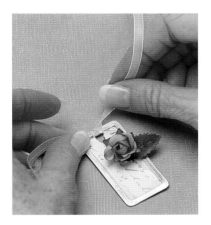

STEP **10**

Glue a silk rosebud to the rectangular vellum tag and tie a pink satin ribbon through the hole.

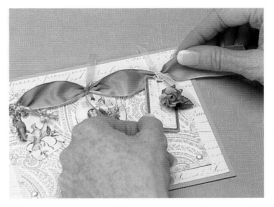

STEP **11** Tie the small price tag, circle tag and rectangular vellum tag onto the blended pink and green ribbon, spacing them equally apart. Trim the ribbon ends at an angle. Glue the ribbon and tags to the card with gel medium.

STEP **12** Ink the tiny alphabet stamps with black pigment ink and stamp the word "printemps" onto a scrap of pink floral print paper. Glue the paper to a piece of ribbed green vellum and tear the vellum around the edges. Glue the piece to the center of the card, below the tags.

CHATEAU OF FLOWERS

THE NAME OF THIS CARD WAS TAKEN FROM an old romance novel that I bought with intent to alter. Its text was so fun that I've used it in several projects. This technique is from the only stamping class I've ever taken (taught by renowned artist and stamp teacher Gaye Medbury). I've adapted it to suit my style and color preferences. With so many layers building up the background, the technique is very forgiving. If something doesn't turn out the way you like, paint or ink over it. Just be sure to let each layer dry before adding another. If you're impatient, get out your heat embossing tool to speed things up.

"I will be the gladdest thing under the sun! I will touch a hundred flowers and not pick one."

EDNA SAINT VINCENT MILLAY

MATERIALS FOR TOP-FOLD CARD

Card: light green cardstock cut to
4³/₄" x 9¹/₂" (12.1cm x 24.1cm),
then folded to 4³/₄" x 4³/₄"
(12.1cm x 12.1cm)

Teal cardstock cut to 4¹/₂" x 4¹/₂"
(11.4cm x 11.4cm)

White cardstock cut to 4¹/₄" x 4¹/₄"
(10.8cm x 10.8cm)

Text from an old book

Seed packet ephemera

One silk flower with silk leaf

One turquoise rhinestone

One oval dimensional sticker

Flower sprig and decorative stamps

Lime green and turquoise chalk
inks

Black permanent ink

Antique Linen distress ink

Embossing ink

Green moss embossing powder

Heat embossing tool

Off-white and lime green acrylic
paints

Cutting, punching and scoring
tools (see page 122 for options)

Adhesives (see page 122 for
options)

SILK FLOWER AND LEAF BY
MAKING MEMORIES ◆ SEED PACKET
EPHEMERA BY PROVO CRAFT
(ALTERED ELEMENTS COLLECTION) ◆
STICKER BY CREATIVE
IMAGINATIONS ◆ STAMPS BY
STAMPA ROSA, RUBBER STAMPEDE
AND STAMPERS ANONYMOUS ◆
DISTRESS INK BY RANGER

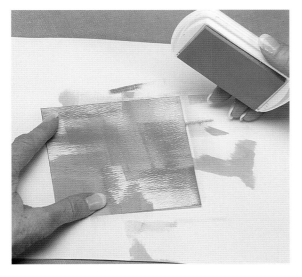

STEP 1 Swipe lime chalk ink over the white cardstock and allow to dry. Repeat with turquoise chalk ink.

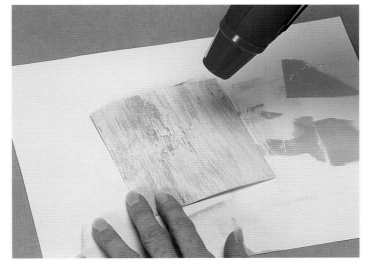

STEP 2 Apply a thin coat of off-white acrylic paint and then wipe off a little of the paint with a paper towel. Dry with a heat embossing tool.

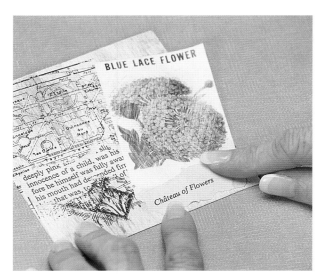

STEP 3 Ink various decorative stamps with black permanent ink and randomly stamp over the cardstock.

STEP 4 Tear text and appropriate phrases from an old book and glue them to the cardstock. Distress the seed packet ephemera as described on page 125 and glue it to the cardstock.

STEP 5 Swipe Antique Linen distress ink onto the text bits and seed packet ephemera.

STEP 6 Drybrush off-white and lime green acrylic paint over the entire collage.

96

STEP **7** Ink the flower sprig stamp with moss green embossing ink and emboss the images as described on page 34, steps 3 and 4.

STEP **8** Glue the collage onto the teal cardstock. Apply the clear oval dimensional sticker over the phrase from the old book.

STEP **9** Glue a silk leaf and flower to the top left corner of the collage and add a turquoise rhinestone to the center of the flower.

STEP **10** Glue the entire layered collage to the center of the light green card.

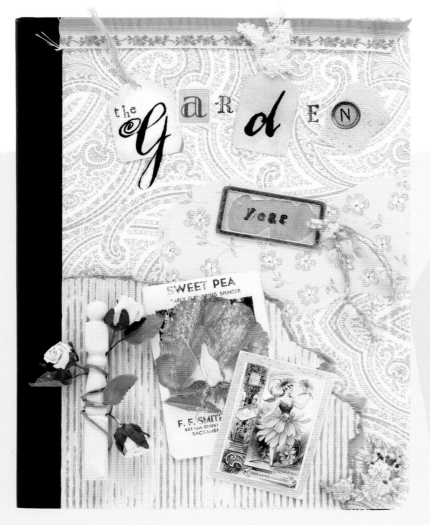

I LOVE TO GARDEN, and I originally envisioned this project as an altered book. I wanted to include thoughts and musings on the different aspects of gardening throughout the year, beginning with planning in February, and moving through all the digging, planting, weeding, watering, blooming and dying of the year. With a composition book base, this project becomes the perfect notebook for a gardener. Everything can be recorded here, from planting ideas and what worked (or didn't) to bloom times and when to take in tender plants. A pocket can be added inside the cover to hold seed packets or loose papers.

"Every flower about a house certifies to the refinement of somebody. Every vine climbing and blossoming tells of love and joy."

ROBERT G. INGERSOLL

MATERIALS FOR JOURNAL

7½" x 9½" (19cm x 24.1cm) composition book

Corrugated cardboard cut to 5" x 7"(12.7cm x 17.8cm)

Green paisley paper cut to 6¾" x 9¾"(17.2cm x 24.8cm)

Pink floral print paper cut to 3½" x 5" (8.9cm x 12.7cm)

Scrap of pink paper

Scrap of ribbed green vellum

Garden-themed ephemera

Two small price tags and one metal rim rectangular vellum tag

Typewriter key and letter stickers

One wooden dollhouse banister

Three pink wired roses

One corner embellishment

Tiny alphabet stamps

Black and green pigment inks

Light green and white acrylic paints

Pink chalk

8" (20.3cm) pieces of pink and green decorative ribbon, embroidered ribbon and green and pink embroidery floss

Cutting, punching and scoring tools (see page 122 for options)

Adhesives (see page 122 for options)

PAISLEY PAPER BY ANNA GRIFFIN, INC • PINK FLORAL PRINT PAPER BY COLORBÖK • WOODEN BANISTER PIECE BY CRAFTS ETC! (SMALL TOWN TREASURES COLLECTION) • GARDEN-THEMED EPHEMERA BY PROVO CRAFT • TAGS BY AVERY AND MAKING MEMORIES • STICKERS BY FLAVIA, EK SUCCESS AND CREATIVE IMAGINATIONS (SONNETS COLLECTION) • TINY ALPHABET STAMPS BY HERO ARTS

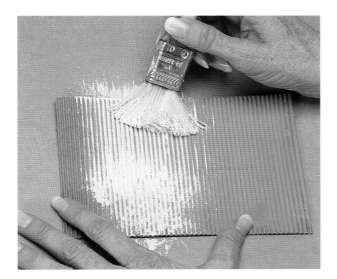

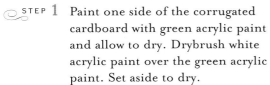

STEP 1 Paint one side of the corrugated cardboard with green acrylic paint and allow to dry. Drybrush white acrylic paint over the green acrylic paint. Set aside to dry.

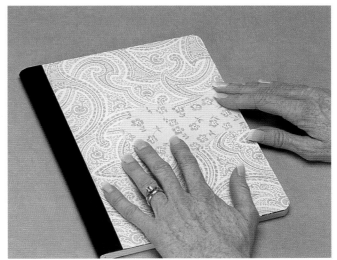

STEP 2 Glue the green paisley paper to the front of the composition book and trim as needed. Tear off and discard three sides of the pink floral print paper and glue the remaining paper to the center of the journal with the untorn side lined up with the right edge of the journal.

STEP **3**   Tear off and discard the top right corner of the painted cardboard. Glue the remaining cardboard to the bottom left edge of the journal. Cut out the sweet pea seed packet and flower fairy image from the garden-themed ephemera. Glue the fairy to a scrap of pink paper. Distress both images as described on page 125, then glue them to the cardboard.

STEP **4**   Paint the wooden doll house banister with white acrylic paint, allow it to dry, then distress it as desired. Wrap a few wired roses around the banister piece.

STEP **5**

Dab white acrylic paint onto the decorative corner embellishment and attach it to the bottom right corner of the journal with gel medium. Glue the embroidered ribbon across the top of the journal.

STEP **6**   Use a cotton swab or foam eyeshadow brush to apply pink chalk to a small price tag. Ink the tiny alphabet stamps with black pigment ink and stamp the word "the" onto the tag. Tie green embroidery floss through the hole in the tag and attach it to the top left corner of the journal. Add a letter "G" sticker to the tag.

STEP 7 Apply the letter "A" sticker to the journal, then stamp the letter "R" with black pigment ink. Smudge a small price tag with green pigment ink and tie pink embroidery floss through the hole in the tag. Apply the letter "D" sticker to the tag and glue the tag to the journal.

STEP 8 Stamp the letter "E" onto the journal with black pigment ink. Apply the letter "N" typewriter key sticker to a scrap of pink paper and glue it to the journal next to the "E."

STEP 9 Stamp or write the word "year" on a scrap of green vellum. Tear out the center of a rectangular vellum tag and glue it over the word on the green vellum. Trim around the edges.

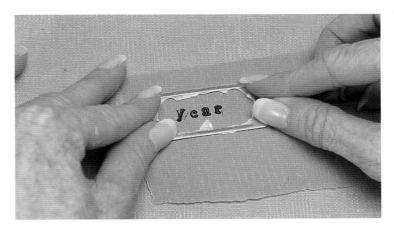

STEP 10 Punch a hole in the vellum with the any-where punch. Tie a piece of pink and green decorative ribbon through the hole in the tag and attach it to the journal with gel medium.

MILESTONES AND MOMENTS

EVERYTHING'S A CIRCLE. EACH YEAR HOLDS THE

annual lineup of holidays, birthdays and anniversaries, even special days

to honor mothers and fathers. Other events, like births and weddings, are

not as predictable, but no less universal.

   It seems to be a natural impulse to mark these important events in

a special way. But do you ever find yourself stumped about how to do

that meaningfully? That's one of the reasons I like these projects.

   Celebrating the milestones in life tends to be fairly straightforward.

Even though it may require a great deal of work, we know how to

"do" birthdays, weddings and holidays. But what about the other

events, all the little stuff that adds pleasure and enjoyment to our

lives? In *O Magazine*, Maria Edgeworth said, "*If we take care of the

moments, the years will take care of themselves.*" I like the idea of paying attention to daily

moments but, truth to tell, don't always manage it. However, wouldn't it be delightful to make special note of things like

the year's first snowfall, your child's great test score, or any other occasion that brings a smile to your face? How about

creating a card to celebrate
these events and share
them with others?

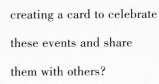

A BABY SO PRECIOUS

A NURSERY IN SOFT COLORS and filled with antiques inspired this pretty card. I tried to capture the feeling of wallpaper for the background. This would be a lovely way to use a treasured family photo or portrait, but be sure to use a color copy and preserve the original. Don't be limited by the palette you see here. By substituting blue striped paper for the pink toile paper, for instance, the card works equally well for a baby boy. You can also spell out the child's name or other nursery-related words such "lullaby" and "hush."

"...to have a child...is to decide forever to have your heart go walking around outside your body."

ELIZABETH STONE

MATERIALS FOR TOP-FOLD CARD

Card: light pink cardstock cut to 5" x 10" (25.4cm x 12.7cm), then folded to 5" x 5" (12.7cm x 12.7cm)

Pink toile paper cut to 3" x 4¾" (7.6cm x 12.1cm)

Script print paper cut to 2" x 4¾" (5.1cm x 12.1cm)

Colored toile paper with little girl image

Color copy of old photograph cut to 2½" x 3¾" (6.4cm x 9.5cm)

2½" x 3¾" (6.4cm x 9.5cm) metal frame

Safety pin and heart charm

6" (15.2cm) pieces of twill tape and khaki checked ribbon

Two decorative buttons

Tiny alphabet stamps

Pink pigment ink

Antique Linen distress ink

White acrylic paint

Cutting, punching and scoring tools (see page 122 for options)

Adhesives (see page 122 for options)

PINK AND COLORED TOILE PAPERS BY ANNA GRIFFIN, INC • SCRIPT PRINT PAPER BY 7GYPSIES • METAL FRAME BY FROST CREEK CHARMS • SAFETY PIN BY MAKING MEMORIES • TWILL TAPE BY WRIGHT'S • RIBBON BY MIDORI • TINY ALPHABET STAMPS BY HERO ARTS • DISTRESS INK BY RANGER

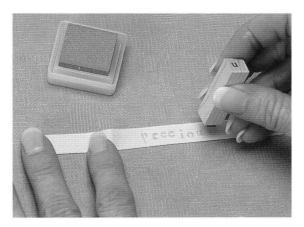

STEP 1 Ink the tiny alphabet stamps with pink pigment ink and stamp the word "precious" onto a piece of twill tape.

STEP 2 Tear out a little girl image from the colored toile paper. Edge the image, script print and pink toile papers with Antique Linen distress ink. Glue the pink toile paper to the bottom and the script print paper to the top of the light pink card. Glue the little girl image to the top left corner of the card. String a heart charm on a safety pin and fasten it to one end of the khaki ribbon. Use gel medium to glue the ribbon over the seam where the papers meet.

STEP 3

Trim the color copy of the photograph to fit inside the metal frame. Glue the frame over the photo, then attach the framed photo to the center of the card with gel medium. Glue the twill tape from step 1 below the frame and add buttons to each side, cutting off the shanks if necessary. Paint the frame with white acrylic paint and wipe off the excess with a paper towel.

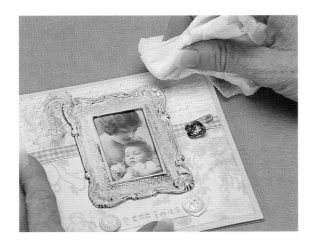

DO WE EVER REALLY GROW OUT OF our delight with birthdays? Even as the years pile up (and up!), it's still fun to have people make a fuss and celebrate our very existence. And of course, there are always presents to look forward to, as well! The baby-faced clown in this card is so charming. She seemed perfect for a birthday card. The pink, black and white color scheme is pulled from the image, as well. It is fresh and timeless—a nice touch for celebrating a birthday. The wavy corrugated cardstock and polka dot ribbon add a playful touch, and the daisy echoes the enormous buttons on the little clown's costume.

"A birthday is just the first day of another 365-day journey around the sun. Enjoy the trip."

AUTHOR UNKNOWN

MATERIALS FOR SIDE-FOLD CARD

Card: white cardstock cut to
10" x 6½" (25.4cm x 16.5cm),
then folded to 5" x 6½"
(12.7cm x 16.5cm)

Black cardstock cut to 4¾" x 6¼"
(12.1cm x 15.9cm)

White wavy corrugated cardstock
cut to 3½" x 4¼"
(8.9cm x 10.8cm)

Pink diamond print paper cut to
4½" x 6" (11.4cm x 15.2cm)

Pink paisley paper cut to 4" x 3½"
(10.2cm x 8.9cm)

Black text print paper cut to
4¼" x 4½" (10.8cm x 11.4cm)

Script print acetate cut to
4½" x 6" (11.4cm x 15.2cm)

Scrap of white cardstock

Clown image

1" x ¾" (2.5cm x 1.9cm) label
holder with brads

One pink daisy

One decorative button

20" (50.8cm) piece of black-and-
white polka dot ribbon

Cutting, punching and scoring
tools (see page 122 for options)

Adhesives (see page 122 for
options)

PINK DIAMOND PRINT PAPER BY
COLORBÖK ◆ PINK PAISLEY PAPER
BY ANNA GRIFFIN, INC ◆ BLACK
TEXT PRINT PAPER BY 7GYPSIES ◆
SCRIPT PRINT ACETATE BY
CREATIVE IMAGINATIONS ◆ CLOWN
IMAGE BY ARTCHIX STUDIO ◆
LABEL HOLDER BY HIRSCHBERG
SCHUTZ & CO ◆ DAISY BY MAKING
MEMORIES

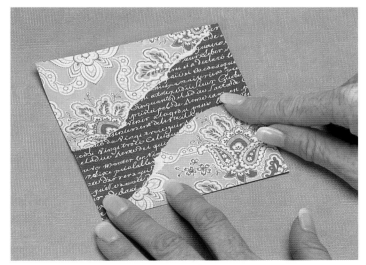

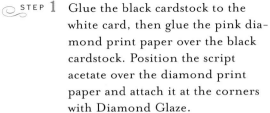

STEP 1 Glue the black cardstock to the white card, then glue the pink diamond print paper over the black cardstock. Position the script acetate over the diamond print paper and attach it at the corners with Diamond Glaze.

STEP 2 Tear the pink paisley paper in half diagonally and glue the top half to the top left corner of the black text print paper and the bottom half to the bottom right corner.

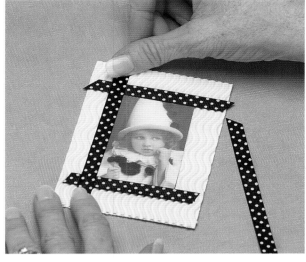

STEP 3 Tear the layered piece from step 2 diagonally just slightly outside the pink paisley corner pieces so that only thin borders of the black text print paper are visible. Glue these pieces to the top left and bottom right corners of the card, overlapping the acetate.

STEP 4 Cut out the clown image and glue it to the center of the wavy corrugated cardstock with double-sided tape. Cut two 5" (12.7cm) pieces and two 4" (10.2cm) pieces of polka dot ribbon and make an overlapping ribbon frame around the clown image, as shown. Attach with gel medium.

STEP 5 Glue the framed clown piece to the top left corner of the card, positioning it diagonally. Glue the pink daisy to the top right corner of the frame with Diamond Glaze. Add a button to the center of the flower, cutting off the shank if necessary.

STEP 6 Print or write the phrase "happy birthday" on the scrap of white cardstock and trim it to the size of the label holder.

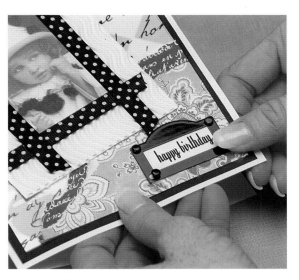

STEP **7** Glue the "happy birthday" piece to the bottom left corner of the card. Position the label holder over the words and mark the holes with a pencil.

STEP **8** Use an awl or sharp tool to pierce the holes and align them with the holes on the label holder. Insert brads into the holes and bend the prongs outward to secure.

ONCE IN A BLUE MOON

This card shows another way to use those cool vintage photos of ancestors, whether real or "acquired." Here, I silhouetted a color copy of an image and tucked it into a frame stamped on patterned vellum. Then, I tore and chalked the edges and added some text and rhinestones for fun!

MY DARLING MOTHER

I CAME UP WITH THIS PIECE when I was trying to think of a project for a class I was teaching. Wouldn't it make an attractive Mother's Day gift? This project lends itself well to variations. Include photos of your own mother at different ages. Or, place photos of each child on a separate tag. Think about your mother's favorite color, flower or hobby, and build the design around that.

"A mother is a person who, seeing there are only four pieces of pie for five people, promptly announces she never did care for pie."

TENNEVA JORDAN

MATERIALS FOR FRAMED COLLAGE

11" x 13" (27.9 x 33cm) wooden frame

Foam core cut to 8" x 10" (20.3cm x 25.4cm)

Cream cardstock

Lavender diamond print paper cut to 2³/₈" x 4³/₄" (6cm x 12.1cm)

Decorative butterfly print paper cut to 2³/₈" x 4³/₄" (6cm x 12.1cm)

Lavender striped paper cut to 2³/₈" x 4³/₄" (6cm x 12.1cm)

Text print paper cut to 2" x 4" (5.1cm x 10.2cm) and 1" x 1¹/₂" (2.5cm x 3.8cm)

Blue butterfly collage paper

Text and botanicals paper

Lace print and ruler print papers

Color copies of old photos or clip art

Three large shipping tags

One decorative brad and eyelet

Game tile and postcard stickers

One slide holder

One 1" (2.5cm) watch crystal

Three small white silk roses

One pearl head corsage pin

Decorative buttons

6" (15.2cm) pieces of pastel and blue fibers, khaki checked ribbon, twill tape and copper tape

2" (5.1cm) piece of crochet trim

Scrap of tulle

White and periwinkle acrylic paints

Copper antiquing solution

Eyelet setter and hammer

Cutting, punching and scoring tools (see page 122 for options)

Adhesives (see page 122 for options)

DIAMOND BUTTERFLY, STRIPED, BUTTERFLY COLLAGE, TEXT AND BOTANICALS AND RULER PRINT PAPERS BY K&COMPANY • TEXT PRINT PAPER BY 7GYPSIES • LACE PRINT PAPER BY KAREN FOSTER DESIGN • CLIP ART BY DOVER • TAGS BY AVERY • WATCH CRYSTAL BY SCRAPWORKS (FRAMES AND HUGZ COLLECTION) • RIBBON BY MIDORI • FIBERS BY SPECIAL EFFECTS (SEA BREEZE COLLECTION) • TWILL TAPE BY WRIGHT'S

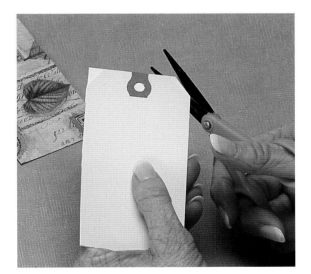

STEP 1 Glue each of the three 2³/₈" x 4³/₄" (6cm x 12.1cm) papers to a large shipping tag, trim around the edges and re-punch the holes in the tops of the tags.

STEP 2 Glue a color copy of an old photo or vintage clip art to the center of the tag that is covered with lavender diamond print paper. Tear out the "violets" definition from the text and botanicals paper and glue it to the bottom of the tag. Fold a scrap of text print paper over the top of the tag and glue it in place, then re-punch the hole.

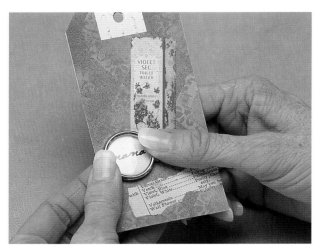

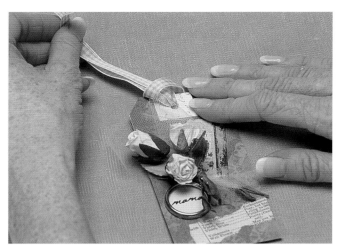

STEP **3** Print or write the word "Mama" on cream cardstock and trim the cardstock to a 1" (2.5cm) circle. Glue the circle to the tag, then press the watch crystal over the circle to indents with the prongs. Pierce holes through the tag at the indents, position the prongs into the holes and bend them inward to secure the watch crystal.

STEP **4** Gather a small cluster of silk flowers, wrap them with tulle and tie the cluster together with the khaki checked ribbon. Trim off the excess ribbon and attach the cluster to the tag with gel medium. Tie a piece of khaki checked ribbon through the hole in the tag and trim the ends at an angle.

STEP **5**

Tear off a 2" (5.1cm) piece of text print paper, wrap it around the center of the tag covered with decorative butterfly print paper and glue in place. Tear out a butterfly image from the remaining butterfly print paper and glue it over the text print paper. Stick the corsage pin through the butterfly.

STEP **6** Glue the blue butterfly collage paper to a slide mount and trim around the edges and window. Print or write the phrase "sweet, sweet mother" on a piece of cream cardstock and glue it inside the window of the slide mount. Trim if necessary.

STEP **7**

Glue a piece of crochet trim across the bottom of the tag, then glue the slide mount over the trim. Antique a strip of copper tape as described on page 79, step 8 and apply it diagonally across the bottom left corner of the tag.

STEP 8 Insert a decorative brad into the hole in the top of the tag and bend the prongs outward to secure. Tie pastel fibers around the brad and trim off any excess.

STEP 9 Apply the postcard sticker to the tag covered with striped paper. Cut out a color copy of another photo and glue it to the tag. Cut a 2" (5.1cm) strip from the ruler print paper and glue it above the photo, then add game tile letter stickers to spell the word "Mum."

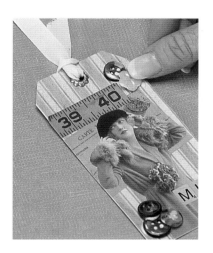

STEP 10

Set a small eyelet through the hole in the top of the tag as described on page 124. Tie a piece of twill tape through the eyelet and trim off any excess. Attach decorative buttons in the lower left and upper right corners of the tag with gel medium, cutting off the shanks if necessary.

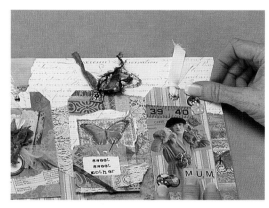

STEP 11 Tear random pieces of your leftover papers and glue them to the foam core with gel medium, making a nice collage. Glue the tags side by side over the collaged paper.

STEP 12 Paint the frame with periwinkle acrylic paint and allow it to dry, then drybrush the frame with white acrylic paint. Insert the foam core collage into the frame.

SONNET FOR A WEDDING

marriage of true minds

THE PHRASES I USED IN THIS PROJECT are taken from sonnets by Shakespeare. As I found out while listening to the radio on his birthday, Shakespeare's words have been set to every type of music imaginable. I could think of no better words than his to mark such a joyous event as a marriage.

This is a triptych piece, meaning there are three panels side by side, hinged together so that the flanking panels fold over the central panel. Don't be put off by the number of steps in this project. Rest assured, the techniques used are not difficult. Just take your time and enjoy it!

joy delights in joy

MATERIALS FOR BOOK

Foam core cut to 5" x 7" (12.7cm x 17.8cm)

One piece of cardboard cut to 5" x 7" (12.7cm x 17.8cm) and two pieces cut to 2½" x 7" (6.4cm x 17.8cm)

One piece of diamond print paper cut to 6¼" x 8¼" (15.9cm x 21cm) and two pieces cut to cut to 3½" x 8" (8.9cm x 20.3cm)

Rose print paper cut to 7" x 9" (17.8cm x 22.9cm)

Two pieces of vintage rose text paper cut to 2⅜" x 6⅞" (6cm x 17.5cm)

Two pieces of ivory embossed paper cut to 3½" x 3¼" (8.9cm x 8.3cm)

Color copy of old photo

Two-piece latch with brads

Four large eyelets

One decorative brad

Several paper roses

One vintage label

Postcard and rose stickers

12" (30.5cm) piece of twill tape

24" (61cm) piece of sheer ivory ribbon

Two 1½" (3.8cm) pieces of lace

6" (15.2cm) pieces of fiber

Flower sprig stamp

Walnut ink in spray bottle

Antique Linen distress ink

Embossing ink and pewter embossing powder

Cream acrylic paint

Eyelet setter and hammer

Cutting, punching and scoring tools (see page 122 for options)

Adhesives (see page 122 for options)

DIAMOND AND VINTAGE ROSE TEXT PRINT PAPER BY AUTUMN LEAVES ◆ ROSE PRINT PAPER BY AMSCAN ◆ LATCH BY KAREN FOSTER DESIGN ◆ DECORATIVE BRAD BY MAKING MEMORIES ◆ PAPER ROSES BY HIRSCHBERG SCHUTZ & CO ◆ LABEL BY MAKING MEMORIES ◆ STICKERS BY 7GYPSIES AND K&COMPANY ◆ TWILL TAPE BY WRIGHT'S ◆ FLOWER SPRIG STAMP BY RUBBER STAMPEDE ◆ DISTRESS INK BY RANGER

STEP 1 Glue the diamond print paper to the large cardboard, cut off the corners of the paper and wrap the sides of the paper around the back of the cardboard. Repeat with the smaller pieces of cardboard and diamond print paper.

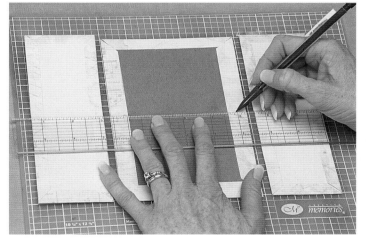

STEP 2 Position the cardboard panels face down, spaced about ½" (1.3cm) apart with the large panel in the center. Mark 1" (2.5cm), 3½" (8.9cm) and 6" (15.2cm) from the top on the inside edges of the side panels and both edges of the center panel.

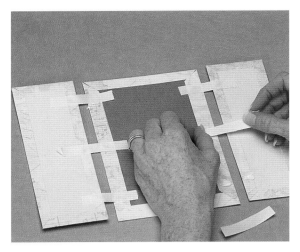

STEP **3** Cut six pieces of twill tape measuring 2" (5.1cm) each. Apply gel medium over the pencil marks and lay the twill tape over the gel medium to make hinges. Allow to dry.

STEP **4** Fold the side panels to the center to make "doors" for your book. Position the latch over both doors where you would like to connect them and mark the placement with a pencil. Re-open the doors, carefully flip the entire book over so that it is face down and use a nail and small hammer to poke the holes for the latch.

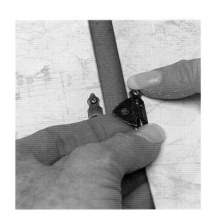

STEP **5**

Flip the book back over, close the doors and attach the latch with brads, bending the prongs outward to secure it.

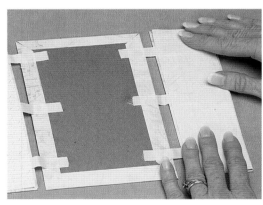

STEP **6** Re-open the doors and cover the inside left and right panels with vintage rose text print paper. Set the entire book aside to dry.

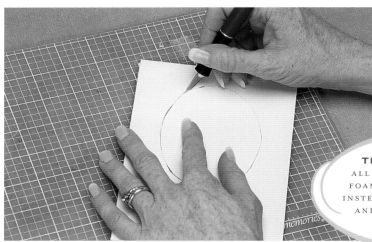

TIP: DON'T TRY TO CUT ALL THE WAY THROUGH THE FOAM CORE THE FIRST TIME. INSTEAD, MAKE SHALLOW CUTS AND SEVERAL PASSES WITH YOUR CRAFT KNIFE.

STEP **7** Cut a 3" x 4" (7.6cm x 10.2cm) oval window out of the foam core with a craft knife.

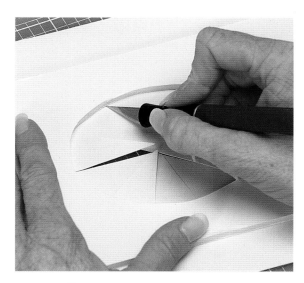

STEP **8** Swipe the rose print paper with Antique Linen distress ink, then glue it to the foam core with gel medium. Use your craft knife to cut the paper inside the window into wedges, like a pie.

STEP **9** Fold the wedges into the window and glue them to the back of the foam core. Trim any paper that extends past the foam core edges, then run your finger along the inside edge of the window to smooth it.

STEP **10**

Apply gel medium to the top and bottom flaps of the paper and wrap them around the edges of the foam core. Repeat with the side flaps. This will make sure the edges are covered and squared off.

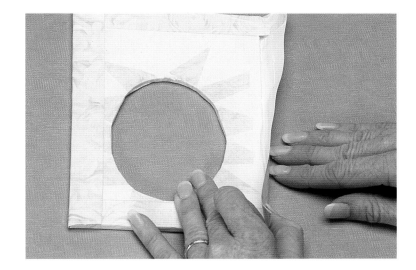

STEP **11**

Cut the excess paper on each corner at an angle.

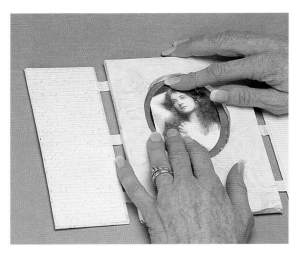

STEP **12** Glue the foam core window piece to the inside center panel of the book. Draw an oval slightly smaller than the window around your photo and cut it out. Glue the photo inside the window.

STEP **13** Spritz some of the paper roses with walnut ink and leave some white. This will create contrast. Glue the flowers inside the window around the photo.

STEP **14**

Place two pieces of ivory embossed paper side by side. Score and fold each piece 2¼" (5.7cm) from the outside edge, as described on page 124.

STEP **15**

Position the scored pieces of paper on the bottom of the foam core and trace the window curves to the top edges of the paper, as shown. Trim as necessary.

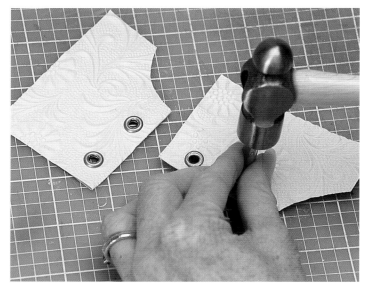

STEP **16** Mark ½" (1.3cm) and 1½" (3.8cm) from the bottom inside edge of each piece of the ivory embossed paper. Punch holes at the marks and set eyelets in the holes as described on page 124. This becomes the book's "corset."

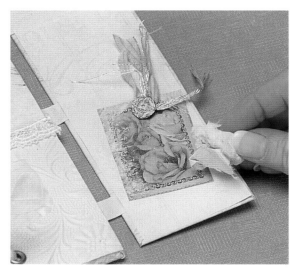

○STEP **17** Glue the outside edges of the corset pieces to the inside panel of the book. Lace the sheer ivory ribbon through the eyelets, tie it in a bow and trim the ends at an angle. Glue small pieces of lace to the tops of the corset.

○STEP **18** Dab a small bit of cream acrylic paint on a decorative brad and dab off the excess with a paper towel. Insert the brad through the top of a rose sticker and bend the prongs outward. Apply the sticker to the bottom inside panel of the right door. Tie fibers around the brad and trim if necessary. Blot a bit more paint onto the sticker with a crumpled paper towel and allow to dry.

○STEP **19**

Apply postcard stickers to the inside panel of the left door and trim off the edges if necessary. Tear the word "rose" from a scrap of the vintage rose text print paper and layer it onto the panel with more rose stickers. Continue layering text, stickers and lace trim on the inside door panels as desired. Allow to dry.

○STEP **20**

Close the doors and fasten the hinge. Ink the flower sprig stamp with embossing ink and emboss as described on page 34, steps 3 and 4. Print or write a marriage-related phrase on the vintage label and swipe it with Antique Linen distress ink. To finish, glue the label across both doors, about 1" (2.5cm) from the top of the book, and use a craft knife to cut it down the center.

GLOSSARY

THE TERMS BELOW ARE COMMONLY USED AMONG SCRAPBOOKERS, COLLAGE ARTISTS AND PAPERCRAFTERS, AND I HAVE USED THEM OFTEN THROUGHOUT THE BOOK.

Acidic: Materials that contain a pH level of less than seven. These should not be used on cards, scrapbook pages and papercrafting projects, as acid will fade and damage photos and other papers.

Acid-free: Also called alkaline, these materials contain a pH level of more than seven and are safe to use for cards, scrapbook pages and papercrafting projects.

Burnishing: Rubbing an image with a bone folder to smooth the surface or attach it to another object

Coated paper: Paper that is covered, or coated, to make it glossy. It does not absorb ink as well as uncoated paper and is generally more expensive.

Collage: Any artistic composition made by gluing various materials of different weights and sizes, such as papers, photos and other embellishments, to a backing material to form an artistic composition.

Corrugated: Depressed with ridges that provide texture, as in paper or cardstock

Distressing: The process of crumpling and uncrumpling, sanding and inking paper, stickers and embellishments to make them look old. (For instructions, see page 125.)

Drybrushing: Applying a thin coat of paint to a surface with a dry brush to create an aged look.

Edging: Coloring the edges of paper or cardstock by dragging them through an inkpad or coloring them with a marker.

Embossing: The process of applying embossing ink to a surface, sprinkling the wet ink with embossing powder and heating it with a heat embossing tool until the powder melts to create a dimensional surface.

Ephemera: Any paper items, such as postcards, ticket stubs or labels, that one might encounter on a daily basis. Typically, these vintage items have been preserved in old scrapbooks. Several companies make themed packages of vintage ephemera reproductions, such as travel or flowers, for use in crafting.

Faux: An artificial representation of something else, such as faux marble or faux wood.

Gloss: The shiny finish that appears on some papers and photos.

Lignin: A naturally occurring, acidic substance in wood that breaks down over time. It should not be used on cards, scrapbook pages and papercrafting projects.

Lignin-free: Materials that contain no lignin and are safe for cards, scrapbook pages and papercrafting projects.

Matte: The dull finish that appears on some papers and photos.

Nonporous: Unable to absorb fluids such as ink.

Patina: A thin greenish layer, usually basic copper sulfate, that forms on copper or copper alloys, such as bronze, as a result of corrosion.

Opaque: Material that is not clear and that light cannot pass through.

pH level: Term that indicates how much acid is in a material. When making cards, scrapbook pages and papercrafting projects, use products with a pH level of seven or above.

Porous: Able to absorb fluids such as ink.

Scoring: Making a line or depression in paper or cardstock to help it fold. (For instructions, see page 124.)

Swiping: Gently running your inkpad over a surface to add color without completely saturating the surface.

Translucent: Material that is clear enough to allow light to pass through.

Uncoated paper: Porous paper, such as newsprint or recycled paper, that has a rough texture and soaks up ink. It is generally less expensive than coated paper.

BASIC MATERIALS

YOU'LL NEED SOME BASIC SUPPLIES TO CREATE YOUR PROJECTS. AS A SCRAPBOOKER, I TEND TO USE MATERIALS THAT ARE GEARED TOWARD SCRAPPING. THE MATERIALS USED IN THESE PROJECTS ARE READILY AVAILABLE IN SCRAPBOOKING AND CRAFT STORES OR THROUGH ONLINE RESOURCES. THE NICE THING ABOUT SCRAPBOOKING PAPERS AND ADHESIVES IS THAT THEY ARE ARCHIVALLY SAFE, MEANING THEY ARE ACID- AND LIGNIN-FREE. REMEMBER THAT MATERIALS CONTAINING ACID AND LIGNIN BREAK DOWN THE CHEMICALS IN PHOTOS AND PAPERS, CAUSING THEM TO FADE, YELLOW AND BREAK DOWN OVER TIME. SO, IF YOU WANT YOUR LITTLE WORKS OF ART TO REALLY LAST, THIS IS YOUR BEST BET.

PAPERS The most basic material for every project in this book is paper. There are several types used in this book.

Acetate: sheet of plastic film that is transparent and usually has a glossy finish; can be used for stamping

Cardstock: heavy-weight paper available solid, flecked or speckled, and smooth or textured; I use 80 lb. cardstock for making the cards—it's sturdy, yet flexible, and supports embellishments well

Foam core: thin layer of foam sandwiched between two sheets of paper; great for adding dimension without adding much weight

Printed papers: lighter weight papers available in every pattern and solid color; common sizes include 8½" x 11" (20.6cm x 27.9cm) and 12" x 12" (30.5cm x 30.5cm), which is common for scrapbooking

Specialty paper: any special paper, such as water color, handmade or soft, fibrous mulberry paper, used to create a variety of decorative and textural effects.

Vellum: lightweight, translucent paper available in variety of colors, designs and textures; can be used over printed paper for a sheer effect

ADHESIVES
I use a lot of different methods to stick one thing to another. Usually, my choice is dictated by the type of material (porous or nonporous) and how heavy or bulky it is. Beyond considering how strong a "stick" you need, there is really no reason to get too hung up on what type of adhesive you use. Unless the instructions in a project specify a particular adhesive, feel free to use whichever one you prefer.

Dimensional adhesive: clear-drying adhesive ideal for gluing glitter, beads, glass, plastic and vellum to paper; dries to a glossy finish; Diamond Glaze is my favorite brand

Double-sided tape: adhesive with two sticky sides, one which is covered with removable backing paper; great for sticking paper to paper

Gel medium: phenomenal gluing agents commonly used by artists to create various textures and finishes when mixed with paint; light-weight gel medium works well for papers, and the heavier gels are especially good for bulky or heavy 3-D items

Glue dots: quick, easy and mess-free dots sold on a roll of paper; available flat or dimensional; work well for sticking items such as buttons or paper together

Glue stick: adhesive handy for lightweight paper-gluing; for papercrafting, look for an acid-free, extra-strength glue stick; the ones intended for kids don't stick well

Clockwise from top: gel medium, glue stick, dimensional adhesive, double-sided tap, glue dots

TOOLS
You'll need several tools for cutting, folding and attaching various items in your projects. Here are some of the basic items I keep in my tool kit:

Anywhere punch: allows you to make a hole anywhere on the paper; sold with several several tips to make holes in different sizes; to use, place the tip where you want the hole on your paper and give the end a tap with a small hammer

Awl: sharp tool used for piercing holes smaller than those made by an anywhere punch

Bone folder: smooth tool with rounded edges and a rounded point at one end; used for scoring, folding and for burnishing (For instructions, see page 124.)

Cutting mat: protects your work surface from damage; self-healing mats don't show blade marks

Craft knife: also called an X-Acto knife, this is ideal for cutting intricate shapes, trimming paper and cutting foam core to size; remember to use a sharp blade, as dull blades are unsafe and can cause accidents

Eyelet setter and small hammer: used to set embellishments called eyelets into paper, cardstock and fabric (For instructions on setting an eyelet, see page 124.)

Heat embossing tool: great for drying paint and ink quickly, as well as for heating embossing powder (For instructions on embossing, see page 34, steps 3 and 4.)

Needle nose pliers and wire cutters: used for bending and cutting wire and removing button shanks

Paint brush: used for applying paint, gel medium and dimensional adhesive to paper and embellishments

Paper trimmer: although this is not necessary for cutting paper, it makes short work of long, straight cuts.

Scissors: used mostly for trimming ribbon and fibers, but also for cutting out images

Sewing machine or needle: great for embellishing cards with decorative stitching; if you don't have a sewing machine, use a needle and thread

Left top to bottom: Scissors, paint brush, anywhere punch, eyelet setter; Right: small hammer

DECORATIVE SUPPLIES AND EMBELLISHMENTS

This is where the real fun begins. Decorations and embellishments give your creations personality, style and texture. Below are some of the many items I used in this book, but for Heaven's sake, don't be limited by this list! Look around and see what else might work. You'll soon be eyeing everyday items in a whole new way.

Acrylic paints: quick-drying paints that clean up with water and are available in every color imaginable

Brads and eyelets: fasteners available in every size, color and shape; brads come with prongs that are bent outward to secure them in place, and eyelets must be set with an eyelet setter and small hammer (For instructions on setting eyelets, see page 124.)

Chalk: adds subtle color to paper; can be applied with a cotton swab or foam eyeshadow brush

Copper antiquing solution: gives a lovely aged, greenish finish, called patina, to copper items such as copper tape; Modern Options makes a kit that includes both the patina green solution as well as the metallic copper "paint," which create antiqued copper accents out of almost anything.

Distress ink: acid-free dye ink, by Ranger, that can be used to achieve a vintage, stained or aged look on photos and papers; rub on directly from the pad or roll on with a brayer

Dye ink: quick-drying, thin, absorbent, water-based ink that is less vibrant than pigment ink

Embellishments: items such as stickers, tags, beads, silk flowers, stamps, markers, metal frames, photographs, ribbon, buttons, game pieces, jewelry findings and matchboxes that add interest and dimension to your creations

Embossing ink and powder: materials that work together to create an embossed, or raised, image (For instructions on embossing, see page 34, steps 3 and 4.)

Pigment ink: slow-drying, thick, vibrant, fade-resistant ink that cannot be absorbed into coated paper; used for stamping, coloring and embossing

Solvent ink: permanent, fade-resistant ink designed for use on plastic, metal, glass and other non-porous and semi-porous surfaces

Walnut ink: great for aging and staining paper and embellishments; available in crystal form, much like instant coffee; to use, dissolve one teaspoon in one-half cup of hot water; I recommend keeping it in a covered plastic container for dipping and painting, or for a less concentrated application, add one part walnut ink mixture with one to two parts water and keep it in a travel-sized spray bottle.

Clockwise from top left: acrylic paints, walnut ink, distress ink, rubber stamp, tags, pigment ink, embellishments, decorative fibers

BASIC TECHNIQUES

ALTHOUGH EACH PROJECT IN THE BOOK REQUIRES ITS OWN UNIQUE MATERIALS AND STEPS, THERE ARE A FEW BASIC TECHNIQUES YOU WILL USE IN SEVERAL OF THE PROJECTS, WHICH I HAVE PROVIDED HERE. PRACTICE THESE TECHNIQUES ON SCRAP PAPER, AND FEEL FREE TO REFER TO THEM IF YOU NEED A REFRESHER COURSE DURING A PROJECT.

SCORING
In order to make a good, clean fold in paper or cardstock, you must make a line or depression with a bone folder. This process, called scoring, is demonstrated below.

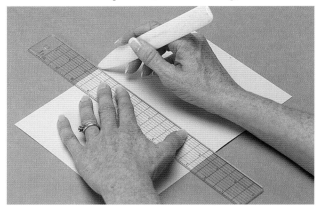

STEP 1 Line up a metal-edged ruler along the center line of the paper. Using a bone folder, "draw" a line along the ruler as if you were using a pencil.

STEP 2 Line up the edges of the paper and fold it along the line. Run the flat edge of the bone folder along the crease to sharpen it.

SETTING EYELETS
Eyelets are metal rings that are great for layering paper and attaching embellishments. They must be set into a hole with an eyelet setting tool and small hammer. There are two types of eyelet setting tools: one for small eyelets and one for large eyelets. To set small eyelets, which are great for use with paper, make a hole with an anywhere punch, then insert the eyelet through the hole. Position the tip of the eyelet setter in the hole and hit the end of the setter with a small hammer. The eyelet edges will curl outward and secure it to the paper. To set larger, two-piece eyelets, which are often used with heavy-duty materials like denim, you must use a small metal rod, a doughnut-shaped base and a small hammer. This is demonstrated below.

SET EYELET
Use an anywhere punch to make a hole where you'd like your eyelet to be. Push the front piece of the eyelet through the hole. Place the eyelet piece (along with the paper) on the metal doughnut. Slip the back side of the eyelet over the shaft of the front piece. Insert the tip of the eyelet setter into the eyelet shaft hole. Whap it a couple of times with a small hammer.

TEARING
Paper tearing is a technique that can add texture, dimension and interest to your projects. It is fast, easy and requires no tools. When you tear your paper, you'll notice that one side of the tear looks a bit more finished, while the other appears to have a rough border. By adjusting your technique, you can take advantage of this to create different looks. Both "rough" and "smooth" tears are described below.

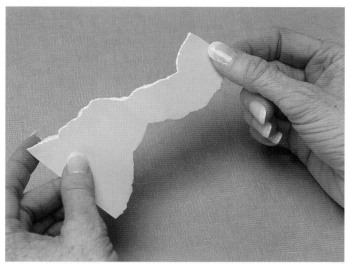

⤳ TEARS WITH SMOOTH AND ROUGH EDGES

Hold your paper in both hands. As you tear, notice that the "smooth" tear (shown here on the bottom edge of the paper) appears on the side of the paper that you pull toward you. The "rough" tear (shown here on the top edge of the paper) appears on the side of the paper that moves away from you as you tear. It doesn't really matter which hand you use. In some instances, it may be easier to flip the paper over so that the "wrong" side is facing you and commence tearing. Try and see what works best for you.

DISTRESSING
Not everyone has access to a treasure trove of authentic vintage letters, papers and photos. I certainly don't. And, I don't really have much opportunity to comb flea markets and antique stores looking for these goodies. Thanks to modern crafting supplies, you can achieve a time-worn look on almost anything—paper, photos, stickers, ribbon—quickly and easily. By sanding, inking and painting, or a combination of these, you can make new-old stuff to use on your projects.

⤳ **STEP 1** Sand the paper with fine-grit sandpaper. Give a little extra attention to the edges and anywhere else you want to appear especially worn. Scruff the edges with your fingernail, or make tiny tears if desired. At this point, you can also create a white-washed look by drybrushing white acrylic paint all over the paper, then wiping it off with a paper towel.

⤳ **STEP 2** Crumple and uncrumple the paper, then "swipe," or gently rub, an inkpad over the surface. The wrinkles will pick up the ink. You can also drag the edges of your paper across the top of the inkpad to vary the look. For instance, using a dark brown inkpad on torn-edged paper will give an aged, almost burned, look.

RESOURCES

7gypsies
www.7gypsies.com

Anna Griffin, Inc.
(888) 817-8170
www.annagriffin.com

ARTchix Studio
(250) 370-9985
www.artchixstudio.com

Art Impressions
(800) 393-2014
www.artimpressions.com

Autumn Leaves
(800) 588-6707
www.autumnleaves.com

Avery
(800) 462-8379
www.avery.com

Colorbök
(800) 366-4660
www.colorbok.com

Creative Imaginations
(800) 942-6487
www.cigift.com

Dover Publications
www.doverpublications.com

EK Success
www.eksuccess.com

Hero Arts
(800) 822-4376
www.heroarts.com

K&Company
(888) 244-2083
www.kandcompany.com

Karen Foster Design
www.karenfosterdesign.com

Li'l Davis Designs
(949) 838.0344
www.lildavisdesigns.com

Making Memories
(801) 294-0430
www.makingmemories.com

Masterpiece Studios
www.masterpiecestudios.com

Midori
(800) 659.3049
www.midoriribbon.com

NRN Designs
www.nrndesigns.com

Paperwhite Memories
(888) 236.7400
www.paperwhitememories.com

Pebbles, Inc.
(801) 235-1520
www.pebblesinc.com

Provo Craft
(800) 937-7686
www.provocraft.com

**Rubber Baby
Buggy Bumpers**
(970) 224-3499
www.rubberbaby.com

Rubber Stampede
(800) 423-4135
www.deltacrafts.com/RubberStampede

Rusty Pickle
(801) 746-1045
www.rustypickle.com

Scrap-Ease
(480) 830-4581
www.scrap-ease.com

Stampers Anonymous
(800) 945-3980
www.stampersanonymous.com

Stampington & Company
(949) 380-7318
www.stampington.com

USArtQuest
(517) 522-6225
www.usartquest.com

"Each friend represents a world in us, a world possibly not born until they arrive."

ANAIS NIN

INDEX

Simply Beautiful Greeting Cards
BY HEIDI BOYD

Whether you're a beginner or a seasoned crafter, *Simply Beautiful Greeting Cards* shows you how to create personalized greeting cards for every occasion. You'll find cards that are great for holidays, birthdays, weddings and "just because." With 50 different quick and easy cards to choose from, you'll be eager to show your family and friends how much you care with style and flair. In addition to the wide array of cards, you'll find a helpful section on basic tools and materials, as well as a treasure trove of papercrafting tips and tricks.

ISBN 1-58180-563-2, 128 pages, #330190-K

Altered Books Workshop
BY BEV BRAZELTON

Books aren't just for reading any-more—they can have windows, doors, drawers and more. *Altered Books Workshop* gives you comprehensive instruction and inspiration for creating multi-dimensional art that is a reflection of your moods, thoughts and life. You'll learn how to turn old books into dazzling works of art by combining mixed media and papercrafting techniques with elements of collaging, journaling, rubber stamping and scrapbooking. You'll love learning the wide range of creative techniques for crafting unique, personalized altered books offered through more than 50 projects and ideas inside this guide.

ISBN 1-58180-535-7, 128 pages, #32889-K

Collage Discovery Workshop: Beyond the Unexpected
BY CLAUDINE HELMUTH

In a follow-up to her first workshop book, Claudine taps into a whole new level of creativity with *Collage Discovery Workshop: Beyond the Unexpected*. Inside, you'll find original artwork and inventive ideas that show you how to personalize your own collage pieces using new techniques and interesting surfaces. In addition, the extensive gallery compiled by Claudine and other top collage artists will spark your imagination. Whether you're a beginner or a collage veteran, you'll enjoy this lovely book both as inspiration and as a practical guide.

ISBN 1-58180-678-7, 128 pages, #33267-K

Creative Craft Lettering Made Easy
BY MARIE BROWNING

This book makes personalizing craft projects as easy as A-B-C! You'll learn how to add your favorite letters, words and sayings to your creations with this fun and easy book that features 15 projects and a wide variety of lettering techniques, including rubber stamping, stenciling, decoupage and beginner calligraphy. Crafters everywhere will give this book an A!

ISBN 1-58180-647-7, 128 pages, #33236-K

These and other fine North Light books are available at your local art & craft retailer, bookstore, online supplier or by calling 1-800-448-0915 in North America or 0870-2200220 in the United Kingdom.